Culture Jam

Culture Jam

HOW TO REVERSE
AMERICA'S SUICIDAL CONSUMER
BINGE—AND WHY WE MUST

Kalle Lasn

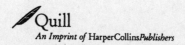

Quill
An Imprint of HarperCollins*Publishers*

A hardcover edition of this book was published in 1999 by Eagle Brook, an imprint of William Morrow and Company, Inc.

HarperCollins books may be purchased for educational, business, or sales promotional use. For information please write: Special Markets Department, HarperCollins Publishers Inc., 10 East 53rd Street, New York, NY 10022.

First Quill edition published 2000.

Designed by Chris Dixon at Adbusters Media Foundation and Michael Mendelsohn at MM Design 2000, Inc.

The Library of Congress has catalogued the hardcover edition as follows:

Lasn, Kalle.
    Culture jam : the uncooling of America / Kalle Lasn. —1st ed.
      p.   cm.
    Includes bibliographical references.
    ISBN 0-688-15656-8
    1. Mass media and culture. 2. Mass media—Influence. 3. Mass media and the environment. 4. Mass media criticism. 5. Popular culture. 6. Social movements.
7. Intercultural communication.
    I. Title.
    P94.6.L37   1999   99–18409
    302.23—dc21   CIP

ISBN 0-688-17805-7 (pbk.)

03 04 05 ❖/RRD 20 19 18 17 16

For my beloved mother, Leida Lasn,
and for Masako Lasn, my partner in life

my teachers Kristjan Lasn,
Fritz Schumacher, Marshall McLuhan,
Guy Debord

my friends Ron Coxhead, Bill Schmalz,
Geoff Rogers, Hideo Iso, Doug Tompkins,
Tadao and Hanae Tominaga

and for my mortal enemy, Philip Morris Inc.,
which I vow to take down

This book was written in a close, intense,
two-year collaboration with my friend
Bruce Grierson. Without his perseverance
and magic way with words, it would never
have seen the light of day.

James MacKinnon weighed in near the
end with a flurry of brilliant ideas.

Ingrid Richardson and Katherine Dodds
were my philosophical gurus. Ryan Bigge
and Paul Shoebridge kept it on the tracks.

Allan Casey, Cat Simril, Charles Dobson,
Sid Tafler, Jurgen Hesse, Jonathon Priddle,
John Mraz, Kyle Frederiksen, Hilary Keever and
Jordan Reeves critiqued the various drafts.

Joann Davis took out all the swear words.

Contents

INTRODUCTION: CULTURE JAMMING

The book you're holding carries a message that your first instinct will be to distrust. That message is, *We can change the world*. It's risky these days to make such a promise because it sounds like one of those meaningless "awaken the inner giant"-type bromides: "If you can dream it, you can do it," "The journey of a thousand miles begins with a single step," and so on.

But it's true. We're serious. We call ourselves culture jammers. We're a loose global network of media activists who see ourselves as the advance shock troops of the most significant social movement of the next twenty years. Our aim is to topple existing power structures and forge major adjustments to the way we will live in the twenty-first century. We believe culture jamming will become to our era what civil rights was to the '60s, what feminism was to the '70s, what environmental activism was to the '80s. It will alter the way we live and think. It will change the way information flows, the way institutions wield power, the way TV stations are run, the way the food, fashion, automobile, sports, music and culture industries set their agendas. Above all, it will change the way we interact with the mass media and the way in which meaning is produced in our society.

We are a very diverse tribe. Our people range from born-again Lefties to Green entrepreneurs to fundamentalist Christians who don't like what television is doing to their kids; from punk anarchists to communications professors to advertising executives searching for a new role in life. Many of us are longtime activists who in the midst of our best efforts suddenly felt spiritually winded. For us feminism had run out of steam, the environmental movement no longer excited, the fire no longer burned in the belly of the Left, and youth rebellion was looking more and more like an empty gesture inspired by Nike. We were losing.

Then we had an idea. Maybe if we banged together the heads of all these activists and reconfigured the fragmented forces of identity politics into a new, empowered movement, we could start winning again.

We weren't looking for it necessarily, but each one of us in our own way has had a political awakening; a series of very personal "moments of truth" about ourselves and how the world works. For some, these insights have come on like powerful, secular epiphanies. Sometimes they have been triggered by things we overheard or read or stumbled upon. Sometimes they have involved things we thought we knew but now, suddenly, *felt.* These truths have left us shaken; it's no exaggeration to say they have changed our lives. I'd like to share with you some of the insights that have occurred to me over the last decade or so.

America is no longer a country. It's a multitrillion-dollar brand. America™ is essentially no different from McDonald's, Marlboro or General Motors. It's an image "sold" not only to the citizens of the U.S.A., but to consumers worldwide. The American brand is associated with catchwords such as "democracy," "opportunity" and "freedom." But like cigarettes that are sold as symbols of vitality and youthful rebellion, the American reality is very different from its brand image. America™ has been subverted by corporate agendas. Its elected officials bow before corporate power as a condition of their survival in office. A collective sense of powerlessness and disillusionment has set in. A deeply felt sense of betrayal is brewing.

American culture is no longer created by the people. Our stories, once passed from one generation to the next by parents, neighbors and teachers, are now told by distant corporations with "something to sell as well as to tell." Brands, products, fashions, celebrities, entertainments—the spectacles that surround the production of culture—*are* our culture now. Our role is mostly to listen and watch—and then, based on what we have heard and seen, to buy.

A free, authentic life is no longer possible in America™ today. We are being manipulated in the most insidious way. Our emotions, personalities and core values are under siege from media and cultural forces too complex to decode. A continuous product message has woven itself into the very fabric of our existence. Most North Americans now live designer lives—sleep, eat, sit in car, work, shop, watch TV, sleep again. I doubt there's more than a handful of free, spontaneous minutes anywhere in that cycle. *We ourselves have been branded.* The human spirit of prideful contrariness and fierce independence has been oddly tamed. We have evolved into a smile-button culture. We wear the trendiest fashions, drive the best cars industry can produce and project an image of incredible affluence—cool people living life to the hilt. But behind that happy mask is a face so ugly it invariably shocks the hell out of my friends from developing countries who come to visit, expecting the giddy Americana depicted on TV and finding instead a horror show of disconnection and anomie.

Our mass media dispense a kind of Huxleyan "soma." The most powerful narcotic in the world is the promise of belonging. And belonging is best achieved by conforming to the prescriptions of America™. In this way a perverted sense of cool takes hold of the imaginations of our children. And thus a heavily manipulative corporate ethos drives our culture. Cool is indispensable—and readily, endlessly dispensed. You can get it on every corner (for the right price), though it's highly addictive and its effects are short-lived. If you're here for cool today, you'll almost certainly be back for more tomorrow.

American cool is a global pandemic. Communities, traditions, cultural heritages, sovereignties, whole histories are being replaced by a barren American monoculture.

Living in Japan during its period of sharpest transition to a western way of life, I was astonished by the speed and force with which the American brand took hold. I saw a culture with thousands of years of tradition behind it vanquished in two generations. Suddenly, high school girls were selling themselves after class for $150 a trick so they'd have cash to buy American jeans and handbags.

The Earth can no longer support the lifestyle of the coolhunting American-style consumer. We have sought, bought, spewed and devoured too much, too fast, too brazenly, and now we're about to pay. Economic "progress" is killing the planet.

This did not fully hit home for me until 1989, when a spate of nightmarish environmental stories suddenly appeared on the news: acid rain, dying seals in the North Sea, medical waste washing up on New York beaches, garbage barges turned away from port after port, a growing hole in the ozone layer, and the discovery that the milk in American mothers' breasts had four times the amount of DDT permitted in cow's milk. In that year a critical mass of people saw the light and became "environmentalists." We were witnessing the specter of a whole planet heading for ruin. To people like me for whom time had always seemed like a constant, eternally moving train which people got on and, seventy years later, got off, it was the end of innocence. The premonition of ecocide—planetary death—became real for the first time, and it terrified me. It still does.

Once you experience even a few of these "moments of truth," things can never be the same again. Your life veers off in strange new directions. It's very exciting and a little scary. Ideas blossom into obsessions. The imperative to live life differently keeps building until the day it breaks through the surface.

When it happened to me I was in my neighborhood supermarket parking lot. I was plugging a coin into a shopping cart when it suddenly occurred to me just what a dope I was. Here I was putting in my quarter for the privilege of spending money in a store I come to every week but hate, a sterile chain store that rarely carries any locally grown produce and always makes me stand in line to pay. And when I was finished shopping I'd have to take this cart back to the exact place their efficiency experts have decreed, and slide it back in with all the other carts, rehook it and push the red button to get my damn quarter back.

A little internal fuse blew. I stopped moving. I glanced around to make sure no one was watching. Then I reached for that big bent coin I'd been carrying in my pocket and I rammed it as hard as I could into the coin slot. And then with the lucky Buddha charm on my keyring I banged that coin in tight until it jammed. I didn't stop to analyze whether this was ethical or not—I just let my anger flow. And then I walked away from that supermarket and headed for the little fruit and vegetable store down the road. I felt more alive than I had in months.

Much later I realized I had stumbled on one of the great secrets of modern urban existence: Honor your instincts. Let your anger out. When it wells up suddenly from deep in your gut, don't suppress it— channel it, trust it, use it. Don't be so unthinkingly civil all the time. When the system is grinding you down, unplug the grinding wheel.

Once you start thinking and acting this way, once you realize that consumer capitalism is by its very nature unethical, and therefore it's *not* unethical to jam it; once you understand that civil disobedience has a long and honorable history that goes back to Gandhi, Martin Luther King, Jr., and Henry David Thoreau; once you start trusting yourself and relating to the world as an empowered human being instead of a hapless consumer drone, something remarkable happens. Your cynicism dissolves.

If cool is the Huxleyan "soma" of our time, then cynicism is its poisonous, paralytic side effect. It is the dark side of cool. It's part of the reason we watch too much TV and don't bother to vote. It's why we get stuck year after year in tedious, meaningless jobs. It's why we're bored so much of the time and become compulsive shoppers.

To find a way out of cynicism is to find a way out of the postmodern malaise. On the far side of cynicism lies freedom. And the pursuit of freedom is what revolutions—and this book—are all about.

The Situationists saw this revolution coming long ago. The French philosophical movement that inspired the 1968 Paris riots predicted what might happen to a society driven by consumer capitalism. The Situationists intuited how hard it would be to hang on to one's core self in a "society of spectacle," a world of manufactured desires and manipulated emotions. Guy Debord, the leader of the Situationist movement, said: *"Revolution is not showing life to people, but making them live."* This instinct to be free and unfettered is hard-wired into each one of us. It's a drive as strong as sex or hunger, an irresistible force that, once harnessed, is almost impossible to stop.

With that irresistible force on our side, we will strike.

We will strike by smashing the postmodern hall of mirrors and redefining what it means to be alive. We will reframe the battle in the grandest terms. The old political battles that have consumed humankind during most of the twentieth century—black versus white, Left versus Right, male versus female—will fade into the background. The only battle still worth fighting and winning, the only one that can set us free, is The People versus The Corporate Cool Machine.

We will strike by unswooshing America™, by organizing resistance against the power trust that owns and manages that brand. Like Marlboro and Nike, America™ has splashed its logo everywhere. And now resistance to that brand is about to begin on an unprecedented scale. We will uncool its fashions and celebrities, its icons, signs and spectacles. We will jam its image factory until the day it comes to a sudden, shuddering halt. And then on the ruins of the old consumer culture, we will build a new one with a noncommercial heart and soul.

It will be an enormous culture jam, a protracted war of ideas, ideologies and visions of the future. It may take a generation or even more. But it will be done. This book is dedicated to explaining how.

Think of *Culture Jam: The Uncooling of America™* as a rebranding strategy—a social demarketing campaign unfolding over four seasons.

In Part One, *Autumn,* we assess the current damages. We begin with a journey through the mental environment, which is sending out the same kind of early warning signals that the physical environment did thirty-five years ago. What does it mean when our lives and culture are no longer shaped by nature, but by an electronic mass media environment of our own creation?

In Part Two, *Winter,* we rough out the problem. America, and much of the rest of the world now, is caught in a media-consumer trance. A numbing sense of commercial artificiality pervades our postmodern era. Can spontaneity and authenticity be restored?

In Part Three, *Spring,* we explore possibilities for renewal. Has the wild American spirit been tamed? Is an oppositional culture still possible? Can we launch another revolution?

In Part Four, *Summer,* we catch a glimpse of what could happen if the American revolutionary impulse reignites.

If it does nothing else, I hope this book gives you pause. Wherever you are, whatever you're doing, I hope it serves as what the Situationists called a *détournement*—a perspective-jarring turnabout in your everyday life.

World War III will be a guerrilla
information war, with no division between
military and civilian participation.

— Marshall McLuhan

autumn

MOOD DISORDERS

Imagine that you are a member of a typical postmodern family, living in a typical house, in a typical neighborhood, in a typical North American city. You're overleveraged and overworked. You eat a lot of takeout, your kids holler for Nikes and the TV is on five hours a day. One day it dawns on you that, as a family, you're failing. You aren't so much a family as five strangers sharing power and water.

You decide, as a tonic, to go on a camping trip—a pit-latrine-and-flame-cooked-wieners experience uncorrupted by phones, faxes or *Baywatch*. In the absence of electronic distractions, you will get to know each other again.

After only a few hours in the wilderness, though, it becomes clear that you don't know how to do this. You might as well have been shot into deep space, so psychologically ill-equipped are you for the enforced camaraderie of the outside world.

Your kids experience actual physical withdrawal from television. Your seven-year-old can't finish a whole sentence or stay focused on more than three bites of her Van Camp's beans. She wears a *Village of the Damned* expression and asks you to repeat almost everything you say.

Your fourteen-year-old finishes his meal in silence and excuses himself to the tent, where he scavenges for magazines and, finding none, just konks out. There are no signs of life. The kids' senses have become so deadened from disuse they can't touch, taste, smell or see that they are in a marvelous place. To them it doesn't feel marvelous. It doesn't feel like anything at all.

If you have read Elisabeth Kübler-Ross, you will recognize that the stages your kids are going through—denial, anger, depression, bargaining—closely mimic the stages of grief, as if they are adjusting to a loss. Which in a real way they are: the loss of their selves. Or rather, the loss of the selves that feel most authentic to them. Their mediated selves. Those selves that, when disconnected from the urban data stream, cease to function.

Your family, like most postmodern clans, finds itself adrift at a historically significant time. The last couple of centuries have marked a radical transition in human lifestyle. We've gone from living in a natural world to living in a manufactured one. For two million years our personalities and cultures were shaped by nature. The generations alive today—who cannot recognize an edible mushroom in the forest or build a fire without matches—are the first to have had their lives shaped almost entirely by the electronic mass media environment.

Most of us are now fully detached from the natural world. We can barely remember the last time we drank from a stream, smelled wild skunk cabbage or saw the stars from a dark remove, well away from the city. We can't remember when we last spent an evening telling stories, instead of having Jerry or Oprah or Rosie tell stories to us. We can't identify three kinds of tree, but we know how much Mike Tyson received for his last fight. We can't explain why the sky is blue, but we know how many times Susan Lucci has been passed over for a Daytime Emmy Award.

This detachment from nature may not seem like much of a problem, but it is. In fact, it's a disaster. In her 1994 book *Bird by Bird*, writer Anne Lamott reflects on a California vineyard in early fall. It is "about as voluptuous a place as you can find on earth: the sense of lushness and

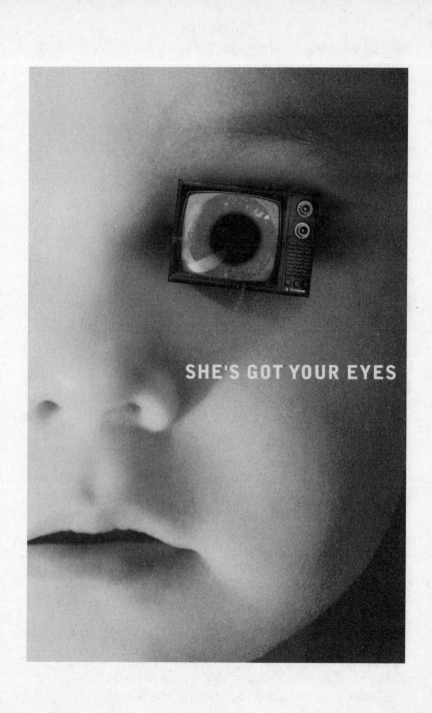

SHE'S GOT YOUR EYES

abundance; the fullness of the clumps of grapes that hang, mammarian, and give off an ancient autumnal smell, semiprotected from the sun by their leaves. The grapes are so incredibly beautiful that you can't help but be thrilled. If you aren't—if you only see someone's profit or that in another month there will be rotten fruit all over the ground—someone has gotten inside your brain and really fucked you up." I think she has it right. Someone *has* gotten into our brains. Now the most important task on the agenda is to evict them and recover our sanity.

Rediscovering the natural world ought not to be difficult. It ought to be an instinctive act. Not just in random bursts of virtuousness should we be moved to replace our divots. If the Earth felt less like something *out there* and more like an extension of our bodies, we'd care for it like kin. We'd engage in what German philosopher Immanuel Kant called "beautiful acts" rather than "moral acts." We'd pull in the direction of global survival not because we felt duty-bound to do so, but because it felt right and good. At a 1990 conference titled "Psychology As If the Whole Earth Mattered" at Harvard University's Center for Psychology and Social Change, panelists concluded, "If the self is expanded to include the natural world, behavior leading to destruction of this world will be experienced as self-destruction."

Sounds promising. But don't hold your breath.

To "ecopsychologist" Theodore Roszak, our rampant, oblivious consumption at the expense of the planet is, simply, a sickness—one no less harmful than the disorders catalogued in the *Diagnostic and Statistical Manual of Mental Disorders* (DSM IV), the encyclopedia of modern psychiatric complaint. It's too new a phenomenon for psychologists to have given much consideration to it.

Roszak views the current widespread sense of malaise as a kind of "separation anxiety" from nature. It should be an easy metaphor to connect with. We're bombarded these days with analyses of failed relationships, of the psychological havoc that breakups wreak. The psychological fallout from our breakup with nature is like that. When you cut off arterial blood to an organ, the organ dies. When you cut the flow of nature into people's lives, their spirit dies. It's as simple as that.

Yet, most of us remain strangers to "beautiful acts."

The postmodern family, out there in the woods trying to bond, can't adapt to real time, real trees and real conversation, because real life has become an alien landscape. Mom and Dad can't navigate in it. No one really feels they belong. No one feels any sense of purpose. The spaced-out daughter is alive when she's in front of the TV, and the mopey son is alive when he's surfing the Net, and Mom and Dad are alive when they're at work. Meanwhile, in real, hairy-ass nature, concrete things keep intruding on their consciousness, breaking their media trance: the rumble of the nearby creek, the prick of mosquitoes on their ankles, the subsequent sight of their own blood.

Living inside the postmodern spectacle has changed people. Figuratively, most of us spend the majority of our time in some ethereal place created from fantasy and want. After a while, the hyperreality of this place comes to seem normal. Garishness, volume, glitz, sleazy excess—the American esthetic H. L. Mencken called "the libido of the ugly"—becomes second nature. "The environment" consists of what you see around you—the ambient spectacle. Occasionally, you'll bump into an outsider bearing tales of that other environment, the one you may have known. When an Inuit elder is asked to draw a picture of the local coastline, he will close his eyes and listen to the sound of the waves on the shore. Such stories seem vaguely ludicrous. Who could be that attuned to the land? More to the point, who'd *want* to be? Where's the purpose in denying yourself civilized amenities when you don't have to?

Once you start asking questions like this, you are, of course, in real trouble. The moment you fail to understand why the natural world might have any relevance in the day-to-day lives of human beings, you become, to quote my old physics teacher, "a lost ball in the high weeds." Abandon nature and you abandon your sense of the divine. More than that, you lose track of who you are.

THE ECOLOGY OF MIND

"Is everybody crazy?" Writer Jim Windolf posed the question in an October 1997 issue of *The New York Observer*, and then answered it himself with numbers.

If you add up all the psychological ailments Americans complain of, the portrait that emerges is of a nation of basket-cases. Ten million suffer from Seasonal Affective Disorder. Fourteen million are alcoholics. Fifteen million are pathologically socially anxious. Fifteen million are depressed. Three million suffer panic attacks. Ten million have Borderline Personality Disorder. Twelve million have "restless legs." Five million are obsessive/compulsive. Two million are manic-depressive. Ten million are addicted to sex. Factoring in wild-card afflictions like Chronic Fatigue Syndrome and multiple chemical sensitivity, and allowing for overlap (folks suffering from more than one problem), Windolf concluded that "77 percent of the adult population is a mess." With a couple of new quantifiable disorders, "everybody in the country will be officially nuts."

His cheeky point is that Americans are turning into annoyingly self-absorbed hypochondriacs. Why? Because they can. Go ahead and cry, says the prevailing psychological wisdom. Any trifling discomfort you might feel has been legitimized. Your pain is valid. If you think you're sick, you are.

There may be a grain of truth to this. People who live in a time relatively free of crises, amidst widespread peace and a galloping economy, will sometimes manufacture crises, inflating minor irritants into major traumas. But surely there's more to the story than that. I think what we have here is a labeling problem. An awful lot of people are feeling down and they don't know why. Something is draining their energy, addling their brains—but they don't know what.

Fact: Worldwide rates of major depression in every age group have risen steadily since the 1940s. Rates of suicide, unipolar disorder, bipolar disorder and alcoholism have all climbed significantly. The U.S. has a higher rate of depression than almost every other country, and cross-cultural data show that as Asian countries Americanize, their rates of depression increase accordingly. Moreover, recent research by the American National Institute of Mental Health confirms that "mood disorders" have increased in each successive generation throughout the twentieth century. I don't usually trust such statistics, but casual observation seems to bear the trend out. Is it just me or is every parent now weighing the merits of Ritalin? Their kids are hyper, unfocused, inattentive. They cannot stay "on task." Mom and Dad aren't faring much better. Tempers are short, attentions wander. Many people—and I include myself in this group—seem to be experiencing higher highs and lower lows these days. We soar the skies one moment, then feel slack and depressed the next.

Why might this be happening? Some researchers blame environmental pollutants: chemical agents in the air, water or food. Others point to cultural and economic factors that are increasing the stress in our everyday lives. No one knows for sure.

But it's tantalizing to guess. In Saul Bellow's novel *Humboldt's Gift*, the narrator wonders how it is that Americans can unashamedly claim to be "suffering," when compared to the rest of the world they are immensely blessed. His answer is that while most people tend to associate suffering with scarcity and deprivation, there's a very different kind of suffering that's caused by *plenitude*.

Plenitude is American culture's perverse burden. Most Americans have everything they could possibly want, and they still don't think it's nearly enough. When everything is at hand, nothing is ever hard-won, and when nothing is hard-won, nothing really satisfies. Without satisfaction, our lives become shallow and meaningless. In this era of gigantism—corporate megamergers, billion-dollar-grossing films and grande lattes—we embrace the value of More to compensate for lives that seem, somehow, Less. Eat the instant you're hungry and, as the Buddhist master put it, "You will never find out what your hunger is for." Plenitude feeds the malaise as it fills the stomach.

In the last quarter century the insatiable craving for the consumer culture's big, big show has only grown stronger. To meet the demand, media spectacles have colonized our mental environment, crowding out history and context. In their place there is now only a flood of disconnected information: The market is soaring, the planet is warming, this fall's hemlines are knee-high, there's a famine in East Africa.

Could it be that all of these things together—the curse of plenitude, the image explosion, the data overload, the hum of the media that, like Denny's, are always awake and bustling—are driving us crazy? I lay my money here. More than anything else, it is our mediated, consumption-driven culture that's making us sick.

Look at the way most of us relax. We come home after work, exhausted. We turn on the TV—a reflex. (If we live alone, we may simply be craving the simulacrum of another human presence.) We sit there passively hour after hour, barely moving except to eat. We receive but we do not transmit. Identical images flow into our brains, homogenizing our perspectives, knowledge, tastes and desires. We watch nature shows instead of venturing out into nature. We laugh at sitcom jokes but not at our spouse's. We spend more evenings enjoying video sex than making love ourselves. And this media-fed fantasy changes us. (Remember the hoodlum Alex in *A Clockwork Orange*, undergoing behavior-modifying aversion therapy via hours and hours of graphic sex and violence on TV? For him the boundaries blurred. "The colors of the real world only become real," he noticed, "when you viddy them in a film.") Layer upon layer of mediated artifice come between us and the world until we are mummified. The commercial mass media are rearranging our neurons, manipulating our emotions, making powerful new connections between deep immaterial needs and material products. So virtual is the hypodermic needle that we don't feel it. So gradually is the dosage increased that we're not aware of the toxicity.

Relatively speaking, this is all very new—too new for its effect on the species to be fully known. We're still adjusting to the all-pervasive media. We are the first two or three generations in history to grow up in a predominantly electronic environment. It took humans thousands of generations to adapt to living on the land (our "natural environment") so it's reasonable to assume it will take dozens of generations to adapt to the new electronic mass media environment that's rapidly replacing the "natural" one. The wild mood swings and the barely repressed anger may simply be symptoms of a shock our systems are experiencing. We are new evolutionary beings, panting for breath on an electronic beach.

We still haven't answered the most basic questions—such as how media violence affects children—let alone the big-picture issues, such as what happens to a whole culture when its citizens start spending half their waking lives in virtual environments. We know there's a correlation between TV viewing and voter apathy (the more TV you watch, the less likely you are to participate in the direct democratic process). We know that TV viewing is linked to childhood obesity (and to the extent that body image erodes self-esteem, we can get an idea of the degree to which TV addiction is harmful to the average child). Beyond that, we're largely guessing. We don't really know what psychological or physiological mechanisms are at work. And because we don't know, to a great extent—and this is the truly odd and scary part—we don't worry much about it.

Ten years ago we didn't think twice about the chemicals in our food or the toxins generated by industry; we thought they were "well within acceptable limits." We were dead wrong about that and today we may be repeating the same mistake with "mental pollution"—nonchalantly absorbing massive daily doses of it without a second thought. Our mental environment is a common-property resource like the air or the water. We need to protect ourselves from unwanted incursions into it, much the same way we lobbied for nonsmoking areas ten years ago.

The antismoking lobby succeeded because people knew without being told that cigarettes were killing their friends and families. They demanded hard data about the risks of breathing in secondhand smoke. They disbelieved glib assurances that cigarettes were safe and that the right to smoke superseded the right to breathe clean air. They trusted their passion and their rage.

More important, antismoking activists changed our idea of what smoking is all about. They uncooled the cigarette companies and their brands, forever connecting smoking and death in all of our minds. It was, perhaps, the first victory in the fight for our mental environment—an ecology as rife with pollutants as any befouled river or cloud of smog. We long ago learned to watch what we dump into nature or absorb into our bodies; now we need to be equally careful about what we take into our minds.

What follows is just a beginning, an introduction to some of the mental pollutants and information viruses we deal with daily—a survey of the threats to our "ecology of mind."

Noise

In 1996, the World Health Organization declared noise to be a significant health problem, one that causes physiological changes in sleep, blood pressure and digestion. It's now understood that noise doesn't have to be loud to do damage.

For thousands of generations, the ambient noise was rain and wind and people talking. Now the sound track of the world is vastly different. Today's noise is all-spectrum, undecodable. More and more people suffer the perpetual buzz of tinnitus—a ringing in the ears caused by exposure to a loud noise (or in some cases, just by aging). One of the treatments for tinnitus is to fit sufferers with a hearing aid that broadcasts white noise. The brain learns to interpret white noise as a background distraction, like traffic sounds, and filters it out along with the tinnitus. The brain works that way for the rest of us as well. The "whiter" the sound in our environment gets, the more we dismiss it as background and stop hearing it. Ultimately, *everything* becomes background noise and we hear almost nothing.

Noise is probably the best understood of the mental pollutants. It's really the only one to which the term "mental pollution" has already been applied. From the dull roar of rush-hour traffic to the drone of your fridge to the buzz coming out of your computer, various kinds of noise (blue, white, pink, black) are perpetually seeping into our mental environment. To make matters worse, the volume is constantly being cranked up. Two, perhaps three generations have already become stimulation addicted. Can't work without background music. Can't jog without a Discman. Can't study without the TV on. Our neurons are continuously massaged by Muzak and the hum of monitors. The essence of our postmodern age may be found in that kind of urban score. Trying to make sense of the world above the din of our wired world is like living next to a freeway—you get used to it, but at a much diminished level of mindfulness and well-being.

Quiet feels foreign now, but quiet may be just what we need. Quiet may be to a healthy mind what clean air and water and a chemical-free diet are to a healthy body. In a clean mental environment, we may find our mood disorders subsiding. It's no longer easy to manufacture quietude, nor is it always practical to do so. But there are ways to pick up the trash in your mindscape: Switch off the TV set in your dentist's waiting room. Lose that noisy fridge. Turn off the stereo. Put your computer under the table. Poet Marianne Moore contends that the deepest feeling always shows itself in silence. I think she's got it right.

Jolts

A noise is a jolt, but a jolt isn't necessarily a noise. In broadcasting terms, a jolt is any "technical event" that interrupts the flow of sound or thought or imagery—a shift in camera angle, a gunshot, a cut to a commercial. A jolt forces your mind to pump for meaning.

In 1978, when Jerry Mander first defined "technical events" in his classic book *Four Arguments for the Elimination of Television*, regular TV programming averaged ten technical events per minute and commercials twenty (public television averaged three to four). Twenty years later these figures have doubled. MTV delivers sixty events per minute, and some viewers, still insufficiently jolted, seek more action by roaming the channels. (Channel-surfers, ironically, are both the cause and the effect of jolt hyperinflation. The more frequently viewers surf, the more broadcasters are inclined to fill their programming with jolts to hold the attention of surfers. And surfers, conditioned to expect ever-quicker jolts, become more inclined to surf.)

Why are jolts so inherently interesting? The behavioral psychologist Ivan Pavlov was among the first to try to explain this. Any stimulus change—any jolt—releases hormones that trigger the biologically encoded fight-or-flight response, vestigial from a time when survival depended on being alert to anything in the environment that happened at faster than normal or "natural" speed. The response was designed to keep us from being eaten by cave bears. It was not designed to keep us glued to our TV sets.

However, most TV programs do just that. They are scripted to deliver the maximum number of jolts per minute (and keep viewers suspended through the breaks). When you watch MTV, you are in fight-or-flight mode practically the whole time. Random violence and meaningless sex drop in out of the blue and without context. "Unlike news reports or thematic TV programs, which usually prepare the viewer for violent scenes," concluded a 1995 study on the psychological aspects of MTV viewing, "the abruptness of music-video cuts tends to have greater shock effect . . . and may have more detrimental influence on the viewer." Much has been made of the way toddlers will sit mesmerized before shows like *Teletubbies*, but put a baby in front of MTV and you'll see the same level of rapture. It's an innate response, one that the industry has been quick to exploit.

In the early 1980s, technological advances changed the way films were made. Up to that point, filmmaking was a painstaking process of finding the organic shape of the story, then developing the narrative by weaving together the components, literally splicing strips of 16mm or 35mm film together by hand. National Film Board of Canada founder John Grierson's adage "Everything is beautiful if you get it in the right order" was understood to be a kind of occupational law. Today, new video-editing techniques allow filmmakers to take shortcuts. If there is a structural problem in your story, well, you can just mask it with a jolt. You can solve a continuity problem by simply bamboozling the audience, briefly scrambling their brains. Story editing has become more and more a process of "jolt management." If you can create enough jolts, you have an engaging film.

That's the premise the commercial media operate on today. Keep the jolts coming. Keep audiences on the edge and sell their attention spans to the advertiser before they regain their bearings. What's a postmodern spectacle after all, if not an array of carefully orchestrated jolts?

Is it possible to have too many jolts? Yes. When the levels rise above a certain threshold, the viewer/listener stops pumping for meaning and just surrenders to the flow, to being both entertained and paralyzed. The narrative of actual life is suspended for the duration of the show.

Perhaps the time has come to quantify the consequences of such mental pollution. If psychologists studied the impact of noise and jolt levels in our mental environment the way biologists research the effects of chemicals in our air, water and food, perhaps we could determine how much our brains can safely absorb. We could then compare the risks posed by different mental environments. We could compare living in Los Angeles with living in Portland, or growing up in North America with growing up in Australia. We could create a "livability" index more accurate than the ones that simply measure greenspace, minimum wage and the number of schools.

With reliable mental-environment indexes, we could rate TV programs and stations by how many jolts per hour they manufacture, how much clutter they dump into the public mind and how this may be affecting our mental health. We could then set new agendas: to reduce, not increase, the number of jolts our brains absorb.

Shock

The average North American witnesses five acts of violence (killings, gunshots, assaults, car chases, rapes) per hour of prime time network TV watched. Such statistics are now more likely to prompt yawns than gasps. They don't mean much if we don't distinguish between types of violence—pro wrestling versus *Goodfellas* versus Indonesian cops clubbing student demonstrators on the evening news. Experts can't even seem to agree on whether violence on TV is increasing. Two recent studies turned up conflicting results, and the head of one research team, by way of explanation, mumbled something about flawed methodology.

So the stats are confusing. That hardly means harm is not being done.

The first agenda of the commercial media is, I believe, to sell fear. What the "news" story of a busload of tourists gunned down in Egypt and the cop show about widespread corruption on the force have in common is that they contribute to the sense that the world is a menacing, inhospitable, untrustworthy place. Fear breeds insecurity—and then consumer culture offers us a variety of ways to buy our way back to security.

As for sex in the media, there seems—surprise—to be as big a bull market as ever. TV programmers know what stops us from zapping the channels: pouting lips, pert breasts, buns of steel, pneumatic superyouth.

TV sexuality is a campaign of disinformation, much like TV news. The truth is stretched, the story is hyped. *If you look like a TV star or a model, a desirable mate will be available to you; if you don't, it won't.* Try telling me that living with that message your whole life hasn't changed the way you feel about yourself.

Growing up in an erotically charged media environment alters the very foundations of our personalities. I think it distorts our sexuality. It changes the way you feel when someone suddenly puts their hand on your shoulder, hugs you, or flirts with you through the car window. I think the constant flow of commercially scripted pseudosex, rape and pornography makes us more voyeuristic, insatiable and aggressive— even though I can't prove it with hard facts.

Similarly, I have no hard proof that daily exposure to media violence shapes the way you feel about crime and punishment, or affects the way you feel about that guy standing next to you at the bus stop. What I do know is that my natural instinct for spontaneity, camaraderie and trust has been blunted. I used to pick up hitchhikers; now I hardly ever do. I rarely speak to strangers anymore.

TV programming is inundated by sex and violence because the networks have determined they are an efficient way to produce audiences. The commercial media are to the mental environment what factories are to the physical environment. A factory dumps pollutants into the water or air because that's the most efficient way to produce plastic or wood pulp or steel. A TV or radio station "pollutes" the cultural environment because that's the most efficient way to produce audiences. It pays to pollute. The psychic fallout is just the cost of putting on the show.

Hype

Advertisements are the most prevalent and toxic of the mental pollutants. From the moment your radio alarm sounds in the morning to the wee hours of late-night TV, microjolts of commercial pollution flood into your brain at the rate of about three thousand marketing messages per day. Every day, an estimated 12 billion display ads, 3 million radio commercials, and more than 200,000 TV commercials are dumped into North America's collective unconscious.

Corporate advertising (or is it the commercial media?) is the largest single psychological project ever undertaken by the human race. Yet for all of that, its impact on us remains unknown and largely ignored. When I think of the media's influence over years, over decades, I think of those brainwashing experiments conducted by Dr. Ewen Cameron in a Montreal psychiatric hospital in the 1950s. The idea of the CIA-sponsored "depatterning" experiments was to outfit conscious, unconscious or semiconscious subjects with headphones, and flood their brains with thousands of repetitive "driving" messages that would alter their behavior over time. Sound familiar? Advertising aims to do the same thing. Dr. Cameron's guinea pigs emerged from the Montreal trials with serious psychological damage. It was a great scandal. But no one is saying boo about the ongoing experiment of mass media advertising. In fact, new guinea pigs voluntarily come on board every day.

The proliferation of commercial messages has happened so steadily and relentlessly that we haven't quite woken up to the absurdity of it all. No longer are ads confined to the usual places: buses, billboards, stadiums. Anywhere your eyes can possibly come to rest is now a place that, in corporate America's view, can and ought to be filled with a logo or product message.

You reach down to pull your golf ball out of the hole and there, at the bottom of the cup, is an ad for a brokerage firm. You fill your car with gas, there's an ad on the nozzle. You wait for your bank machine to spit out money and an ad pushing GICs scrolls by in the little window. You drive through the heartland and the view of the wheatfields is broken at intervals by enormous billboards. Your kids watch Pepsi and Snickers ads in the classroom. (The school has made the devil's bargain of accepting free audiovisual equipment in exchange for airing these ads on "Channel One.") You think you've seen it all, but you haven't. An Atlanta-based marketing firm announces plans to send an inflatable billboard filled with corporate logos into geostationary orbit viewable every night like a second moon. British sprinter Linford Christie appears at a press conference with little panthers replacing the pupils of his eyes, where his sponsor's logo has been imprinted on specially made contact lenses. New York software engineers demonstrate a program that turns your cursor into a corporate icon whenever you visit a commercial site. A Japanese schoolboy becomes a neon sign during his daily two-hour subway commute by wearing a battery-powered vest promoting an electronics giant. Administrators in a Texas school district announce plans to boost revenues by selling ad space on the roofs of the district's seventeen schools—arresting the attention of the fifty-eight million commercial jet passengers who fly into Dallas each year. Kids tattoo their calves with swooshes. Other kids, at raves, begin wearing actual bar codes that other kids can scan, revealing messages such as "I'd like to sleep with you." A boy named David Bentley in Sydney, Australia, literally rents his head to corporate clients, shaving a new ad into his hair every few weeks. ("I know for sure that at least two thousand teenagers at my high school will read my head every day to see what it says," says the young entrepreneur. "I just wish I had a bigger head.") You pick up a banana in the supermarket and there, on a little sticker, is an ad for the new summer blockbuster at the multiplex. ("It's interactive because you have to peel them off," says one ad executive of this new delivery system. "And people look at ten pieces of fruit before they pick one, so we get multiple impressions.") Boy Scouts in the U.K. sell corporate ad space on their merit badges. An Australian radio station dyes its logo on two million eggs. IBM beams its logo onto clouds above San Francisco with a scanning electron microscope and a laser— the millennial equivalent of Commissioner Gordon summoning Batman to the Batcave. (The image is visible from ten miles away.) Bestfoods unveils plans to stamp its Skippy brand of peanut butter onto the crisp tabula rasa of a New Jersey beach each morning at low tide, where it will push peanut butter for a few hours before being washed away by the waves. (The company is widely commended for its environmental responsibility.) Coca-Cola strikes a six-month deal with the Australian postal service for the right to cancel stamps with a Coke ad. A company called VideoCarte installs interactive screens on supermarket carts so that you can see ads while you shop. (A company executive calls the little monitors "the most powerful micromarketing medium available today.")

A few years ago, marketers began installing ad boards in men's washrooms on college campuses, at eye level above the urinals. From their perspective, it was a brilliant coup: Where else is a guy going to look? But when I first heard this was being done, I was incensed. One of the last private acts was being co-opted. "What's been the reaction on campus?" I asked the reporter who told me the story. "Not much reaction," he said. It became apparent, as these ad boards began springing up in bars and restaurants, and just about anywhere men stand to pee, that not only did guys not share my outrage, they actually welcomed a little diversion while nature took its course.

This flood of psycho-effluent is spreading all around us, and we love every minute of it. The adspeak means nothing. It means worse than nothing. It is "anti-language" that, whenever it runs into truth and meaning, annihilates it.

There is nowhere to run. No one is exempt and no one will be spared. In the silent moments of my life, I often used to hear the opening movement of Beethoven's Ninth Symphony play in my head. Now I hear that kid singing the Oscar Meyer Wiener song.

Unreality

At a recent Adbusters Media Foundation office party, two young guys walked in the door, grabbed a beer and went straight to the computers, where they surfed the Net for two hours. Except for a few minutes here and there when people came up behind them and commented on something, they had no social interaction whatsoever. I know these guys. They are both very bright. They'd score well up there on IQ tests.

But I wondered how they'd score on a "reality index"—which I define as the ratio of time spent in a virtual versus a "real" environment. The measurement is easy enough to calculate. Jot down in a notebook the number of times a day you laugh at real jokes with real people in real situations against the number of times you laugh at media-generated jokes, the amount of sex you have against the amount of sex you watch, and so on.

As psychoenvironmental indexes go, it might be quite revealing.

We face more and more opportunities and incentives to spend time in cyberspace or to let the TV do the thinking. This is "unreality": a mediated world so womblike and seductive, it's hard not to conclude it's a pretty nice place to be. In that world of unreality, it's easy to forget you're a citizen and that the actual world is an interactive place. The other day as I sat staring at my toaster, waiting for a bagel to pop up, I suddenly felt as if I was about to receive a jolt. There's a kind of internal "clock" that people who work with computers develop. There's a finite amount of time you're allowed to be still and silent (before, for example, the screensaver kicks in), so you develop a sixth sense that tells you when that time is up. It occurred to me, looking at the toaster, that I had not moved a mouse or a cursor for about a minute, and I had the distinct feeling I was about to be "dumped" off-line. I was going to lose my connection. Then the bagel popped up, jarring me back to the sensory world. The smell reached my nose and I thought of the old Woody Allen line, in a paraphrase: Whatever you think of reality, it's still the only place to get a good toasted bagel.

Erosion of Empathy

A wave of shock is striking society that is so new we don't yet have a name for it. It was concocted by advertisers who saw that consumers had become too jaded and media-savvy to respond to mere sexual titillation or intellectual games. The new shock ads go straight to the soul. They aren't clever or coy so much as deeply, morbidly unsettling. *Advertising Age* columnist Bob Garfield calls them "advertrocities." Benetton's dying AIDS patients and dead Bosnian soldiers. Calvin Klein models drowsing in shooting galleries with hunted, heroin-hollowed eyes. Diesel jeans' cryptic "ads within ads," set in North Korea, featuring images of skinny models on the side of a bus packed with (presumably) starving, suffering locals. ("There's no limit to how thin you can get," says the ad on the bus.)

I think these ads are operating on a deeper level than even the advertisers themselves know or understand. Their cumulative effect is to erode our ability to empathize, to take social issues seriously, to be moved by atrocity. They inure us to the suffering (or joy) of other people. They engender an attitude of malaise toward the things that make us most human. We pretend not to care as advertisers excavate the most sacred parts of ourselves, and we end up actually not caring.

The first time we saw a starving child on a late-night TV ad, we were appalled. Maybe we sent money. As these images became more familiar though, our compassion evaporated. Eventually, these ads started to repulse us. Now we never want to see another starving child again. Our sensitivity to violence has been eroded by the same process of attrition; likewise our sexual responsiveness.

There was a time when Claudia Schiffer in her Guess? jeans got our attention. Now she and her supermodel ilk hardly raise an eyebrow, and real people look downright asexual. The motherboard of our libido has been reseeded.

This blunting of our emotions is a self-perpetuating process. The more our psyches are corroded, the more desensitized we become to the corrosive. The more indifferent we become, the more voltage it takes to shock us. On it goes, until our minds become a theater of the absurd, and we become shockproof.

Information Overload

There is more information in the Sunday *New York Times* than the average person living during the Renaissance would have absorbed in a lifetime. The information glut, the so-called data smog hanging low in the valleys, calls to mind the bewildered student's lament: "I don't need to know any more—I already know more than I can understand." Information overload gave William Gibson's Johnny Mnemonic something called the "black shakes." That's a science fiction conceit, but anyone who ever bought a satellite dish or logged onto the Lexis/Nexis database can surely identify.

"Most information has long stopped being useful for us," wrote Neil Postman, the author of *Amusing Ourselves to Death*. "Information has become a form of garbage. It comes indiscriminately—directed at no one in particular, disconnected from usefulness; we are swamped by information, have no control over it and do not know what to do with it. And the reason we don't is that we no longer have a coherent conception of ourselves, our universe and our relation to one another and our world. We do not know where we came from, where we are going or why we are going there. We have no coherent framework to direct our definition of our problems or our search for their solutions. Therefore, we have no criteria for judging what is meaningful, useful, or relevant information. Our defenses against the information glut have broken down; our information immune system is inoperable."

Infotoxins

If we now absorb a surreal quantity of information, then the *quality* of that information is even more disturbing. The reality presented to us by the media always has a spin on it. Ads stretch the truth, news bites give only part of the story, and White House press releases are carefully tailored to make the president look good. We are constantly being hyped, suckered and lied to.

The marketers, spin doctors and PR agents who produce this propaganda realize what we as a society hate to admit: Disinformation works.

Do an overwhelming number of respected scientists believe that human actions are changing the Earth's climate? Yes. OK, that being the case, let's undermine that by finding and funding those few contrarians who believe otherwise. Promote their message widely and it will accumulate in the mental environment, just as toxic mercury accumulates in a biological ecosystem. Once enough of the toxin has been dispersed, the balance of public understanding will shift. Fund a low-level campaign to suggest that any threat to the car is an attack on personal freedoms. Create a "grassroots" group to defend the right to drive. Portray anticar activists as prudes who long for the days of the horse and buggy. Then sit back, watch your infotoxins spread—and get ready to sell bigger, better cars for years and years to come.

Can we come up with antidotes to these infoviruses that infect our minds? The answer may depend on how much we've ingested of the most powerful and persistent infotoxin of them all: cynicism.

Loss of Infodiversity

Information diversity is as critical to our long-term survival as biodiversity. Both are parts of the bedrock of human existence. And so, when one man gains control of more than half a country's daily newspapers (as is the case with Conrad Black in Canada), or amasses a global media empire the size of Rupert Murdoch's, it's a serious problem; the scope of public discourse shrinks. When a handful of media megacorporations control not only the daily newspapers and TV airwaves but the magazine, book publishing, motion picture, home video and music industries as well, information and cultural diversity both plummet.

A 1998 survey of eleven- to fifteen-year-old boys and girls in a school in Kathmandu revealed that their favorite TV program was MTV and the most popular radio station was Hits FM, a western music channel. Few of the students ever watched Nepal Television or India's *Doordarshan.* In a dozen Asia-Pacific countries surveyed by the A. C. Nielsen company the same year, Coke was the favorite drink in eleven (in Thailand, the favorite drink was Pepsi). In downtown London, Bangkok,

Tokyo or Los Angeles, you will invariably see a McDonald's restaurant on one corner, a Benetton store on the other and a bunch of transnational corporate logos across the street.

Cultural homogenization has graver consequences than the same hairstyles, catchphrases, music and action-hero antics perpetrated *ad nauseam* around the world. In all systems, homogenization is poison. Lack of diversity leads to inefficiency and failure. The loss of a language, tradition or heritage—or the forgetting of *one good idea*—is as big a loss to future generations as a biological species going extinct.

An Environmental Movement of the Mind

"There was once a town in the heart of America where all life seemed to live in harmony with its surroundings . . . Then a strange blight crept over the area and everything began to change."

The fictitious town that fell prey to this "strange illness" in Rachel Carson's famous environmental manifesto *Silent Spring* is a kind of Everytown, U.S.A. Once there was fecundity and the happy buzz of diverse life. Then human intervention caught up with nature. In this quiet season, no chicks hatched. The cattle and sheep sickened and died. No birds returned; the farmers spoke of much illness in their families. "It was," Carson says, "a spring without voices."

No witchcraft, no enemy action or natural catastrophe silenced the rebirth of new life in this stricken world. The people did it themselves— with chemicals and pesticides.

The language and the metaphors Carson used thirty years ago apply equally well to the mental environment we have created for ourselves today. A single voice fills Everytown now; at its say-so, all the sheep lie down in sync. Life in this stricken, alien world has not so much been silenced as reengineered.

We cannot continue polluting our minds. We cannot allow advertisers to continue preying on our emotions. We cannot allow a handful of media conglomerates to seize control of the global communications superstructure. *Silent Spring* and other books and documentaries of its time shocked us into realizing that our natural environment was dying, and catalyzed a wave of activism that changed the world. Now it's time to do the same for our mental environment.

MEDIA VIRUS

Twenty-five years ago, when the world had not quite lost all of its innocence and idealism, I was living in a film commune, churning out experimental films—short five- to ten-minute cultural commentaries. All the members of our commune were fascinated with film and its seemingly magical power to change the world. We showed our shorts to small groups around the Pacific Northwest for a couple of years, but yearned for wider exposure. It occurred to us to condense some of our most incisive efforts into thirty- and sixty-second TV spots and air them as paid "uncommercial" messages. In those days, a local thirty-second timeslot after midnight cost only about $50. Even we could afford that. I walked into the network headquarters of the Canadian Broadcasting Corporation with a few hundred dollars in my pocket and tried to buy some airtime. The sales department was on the second floor of a tawdry downtown Vancouver building. I remember feeling intimidated and eventually being laughed out of the office. "I don't know what this is," the manager in charge of sales told me as he looked over our storyboards, "but it's not a commercial."

I thought it was strange that a citizen willing to pay couldn't buy airtime on Canada's public broadcasting system. I sent a letter to the Canadian Radio-Television and Telecommunications Commission— Canadian broadcasting's governing body—asking about the rights of citizens to access the public airwaves. I got a very polite letter back saying basically that the whole area was murky, that networks had some rights, individuals had some rights, the law was inconclusive on this point, blah, blah, blah. And that was that. I moved on to a career in documentary filmmaking and the free speech issue slipped to the back of my mind—until 1989.

That year, British Columbia's logging industry, its image rapidly tarnishing, launched a multimillion-dollar PR campaign. Bus-stop posters went up all over Vancouver, and every night when I switched on my TV there was another smooth pitch explaining the wonderful job the industry was doing managing the forests. This slick series of spots, produced by one of the biggest ad agencies in town, always ended with the upbeat reassurance that we British Columbians need have no fear. Our forests were in good hands, they were being well managed, and we would have "Forests Forever." This slogan spread like an infovirus throughout the province.

Those British Columbians who knew what was really happening in the forests were livid. The industry was blatantly lying. In truth, the forests of B.C. and the Pacific Northwest have a history of appalling management. For years the timber companies (whose executives held the view that a tree is just an unemployed log) cut too much old-growth too quickly and without proper public consultation. Consequently, the hills were scarred with clear-cuts, and salmon runs were contaminated and dying. There had been mass demonstrations and civil disobedience to stop this liquidation of the Earth's richest temperate rain forests.

So a group of us—including myself, wilderness cinematographer Bill Schmalz and half a dozen other environmental activists—came up with our own campaign. "Mystical Forests" tried to tell the other side of the story: The industry was logging at an unsustainable rate and the future of forestry in our province was in jeopardy.

When we tried to buy airtime for our ad, the TV stations turned us down. At the CBC, the same sales manager who had laughed me out of his office fifteen years earlier again wouldn't take our money (this time he did not laugh). He refused "Mystical Forests" even while he continued to sell airtime to the "Forests Forever" campaign. It seemed ludicrous, undemocratic, and it made us furious.

We mobilized in retaliation. We issued press releases, hounded journalists and protested in front of forest company headquarters. There were editorials in the local papers, TV news coverage, appearances on radio talk shows—and suddenly the forest company executives were backpedaling. Their promise of "Forests Forever" caved in under scrutiny. We popped their multimillion-dollar PR bubble right in their faces and suddenly the CBC was on the defensive as well. Hundreds of British Columbians phoned the CBC's head office demanding to know why environmentalists couldn't buy airtime whereas the forest industry could.

A few weeks later, unexpectedly, the CBC had a change of heart. They never did air our spot, but they pulled the "Forests Forever" campaign—a major loss of face for the industry and a big boost for the environmentalists. Many British Columbians—some for the first time—started having doubts about what was really happening in their forests, and, more to the point, started seriously questioning what was being sold on TV as truth.

We'd beaten the forest industry at its own game—on a budget of zero. We felt euphoric, and that heady mood gave birth to the Adbusters Media Foundation (usually just called Adbusters or the Media Foundation). We decided to produce more TV campaigns about the seminal issues of our time, and to insist on our right to purchase commercial airtime for those issues. We also launched the media activist networking magazine *Adbusters*, and, a little later, the *Culture Jammer's Campaign Headquarters* on the World Wide Web (www.adbusters.org).

We produced the "Autosaurus" TV campaign (a takedown of the auto industry involving a rampaging dinosaur made of scrap cars), "Obsession Fetish" (a critique of the fashion industry featuring a bulimic Kate Moss look-alike), "TV Turnoff Week" (a yearly campaign encouraging TV abstinence) and "Buy Nothing Day"—and all of them were systematically, repeatedly rejected by not only the CBC but by all the North American TV networks, including the big three: NBC, CBS and ABC. (CNN would eventually air the "Buy Nothing Day" ad, but only after a pit bull terrier of a *Wall Street Journal* reporter put pressure on the network to justify its refusal.) Now, these are not crummy low-budget commercials that offended the networks' delicate sensibilities. They're effective and professional. The networks could not and did not object to how they looked. They objected to what they said.

And the stonewalling continues to this day.

Sometimes the hypocrisy is maddeningly blatant. Every Christmas season, the airwaves are full of consumption messages as our culture embarks on another whirlwind buying binge. But year after year the big three networks have refused to sell us airtime for our "Buy Nothing Day" announcement.

Over the years, I've spent dozens of hours arguing with the network executives about why they're censoring us. Here's what some of them have had to say in their own defense:

> *"There's no law that says we have to air anything—we'll decide what we want to air or not."*
> —ABC New York station manager Art Moore

> *"We don't want to take any advertising that's inimical to our legitimate business interests."*
> —NBC network commercial clearance manager Richard Gitter

> *"I dare you to get any station manager in this town to air your message."*
> —CBS network's Libby Hawkins in New York

> *"We don't sell airtime for issue ads because that would allow the people with the financial resources to control public policy."*
> —CBS Boston public affairs manager Donald Lowery

"This commercial ["Buy Nothing Day"] . . . *is in opposition to the current economic policy in the United States."*
—CBS network's Robert L. Lowary

I get a creepy sense of *déjà vu* listening to remarks like that. I was born in Estonia, where for fifty years during Soviet rule people were not allowed to speak up against the government. There simply were no media channels for debating controversial public issues because the government did not want such discussion to take place. Soviet dissidents used to talk about a "public sphere of discourse" that was missing from their country. The oppression of that era was rightly decried. Ultimately, a lot of Westerners watched the Soviet Union fall apart with some sense of vindication.

In North America today there's a similar public void. There's a lack of media space in which to challenge consumptive, commercial and corporate agendas. In the former Soviet Union you weren't allowed to speak out against the government. In North America today you cannot speak out against the sponsors.

This inability to speak up, this public information void, extends across all media at every level. Young reporters who cut their teeth on small-town newspapers invariably swap stories about how they ran into a wall the moment they tried to do real investigative work. The tales often go something like this: There's a smelter or a pulp mill on the outskirts of town. It employs a lot of the townsfolk and donates a lot of money to good causes. Unfortunately, it's an environmental nightmare: For years it's been dumping heavy metals into streams and poisoning the aquifer. The reporter tries to ferret out the facts. She calls the company's media liaison, who blows her off. She calls up that guy's boss, who fails to call back. The next day the publisher takes the reporter into her office and tells her to drop the story. "That company is an esteemed member of the community," she says. "Every year they buy a huge color supplement, and they host the annual summer barbecue that all the other advertisers attend. So just drop it. There are plenty of other things to write about. Look: They're painting the tennis courts tomorrow. Go find the essential drama in *that* story."

And up the chain it goes.

The looming presence of big advertisers influences, if only subconsciously, every executive decision made in every newsroom across North America. Ninety percent of news editors surveyed in a 1992 Marquette University study said they'd experienced "direct pressure" from advertisers trying to influence content; more than a third admitted they had, at some point, caved in and done what the advertisers wanted. Important advertisers are stroked with "soft" pieces designed to move product while important stories are buried.

The most high-minded, ethically intentioned networks and publications are not above striking Faustian pacts.

The PBS flagship *NewsHour*, which is underwritten by Archer Daniels Midland, conveniently ignored the agribusiness giant's price-fixing scandal throughout 1995.

The New Yorker magazine recently cut a deal with Crystal Cruises, wherein the magazine agreed to send seven of its high-profile writers and editors on a world cruise aboard a Crystal cruiseliner (the staffers are required to give some on-board lectures). Its back thus scratched, Crystal agreed to buy six full pages of ad space in the magazine, and it promptly began promoting the cruise ("*The New Yorker* Goes to Sea!"), aiming its ads at rich travelers hoping to gain a little wit and sophistication by osmosis.

Where will all this dirty dancing eventually lead us? The answer may lie in cyberspace, where objective "news" stories already feature hypertext links to advertising merchants. Book giant Barnes & Noble pays *The New York Times* and the *Los Angeles Times* to send readers who click on highlighted titles directly to the store's virtual headquarters (where they can order the book themselves).

With this precedent set, many observers predict the full infiltration of commercial forces into all on-line content. You'll read an obituary of country crooner John Denver and grow nostalgic. But here's relief: Double-click on "Rocky Mountain High" and you'll find yourself at the virtual headquarters of the record company selling a boxed set of Denver's greatest hits. You like the sound of a company mentioned in a business story on Silicon Valley start-ups? Why not buy the stock from this on-line brokerage house? Just double-click here.

In 1997, Chrysler, one of the five largest advertisers in the U.S., sent letters to one hundred newspaper and magazine editors demanding to review their publications for stories that could prove damaging or controversial. "In an effort to avoid potential conflicts, it is required that Chrysler corporation be alerted in advance of any and all editorial content that encompasses sexual, political, social issues or any editorial content that could be construed as provocative or offensive." According to a spokesperson at Chrysler, every single letter was signed in agreement and returned. This kind of editorial control is widely, quietly practiced throughout the industry.

In today's media environment, advertisers rule—the sponsor is king. That ideology is now so entrenched within media circles as to have become an unspoken operational code. Lessons about power, privilege and access are learned at the lower levels by young writers who take this received wisdom with them as they move up the media ladder. From the smallest community weeklies to the big city and national dailies, from *Forbes* and *Details* and *Cosmo* to the NBC, ABC and CBS networks, our whole social communications system is rotten to the core.

THE MANCHURIAN CONSUMER

On *America's Funniest Home Videos*, two young men set up a high bench under the basketball hoop. Then one of them comes racing into the frame, leaps off the bench, stuffs the ball and exits stage left, triumphant. The second fellow tries to repeat the feat, with less luck. He barrels in, misses his footing and straddles the bench, hard. There is a roar of laughter. People in the studio audience are literally doubled over with mirth. You suddenly realize you're chuckling too.

But what, exactly, is so funny? The pratfall was hardly surprising: Groin injuries are the very denominator of this show. It's not Buster Keaton material. In fact, the stunt was so obviously set up, the hapless kid so obviously a dupe sacrificed at the altar of brief nationwide TV exposure that the authentic response should probably have been pity. Or shame.

And yet you laughed. You laughed because all the cues told you to. The laugh track and the audience reaction shot double-teamed you. Mostly, you laughed because some network executive in a corner office in Burbank gets paid $500,000 a year to make sure you do. You laughed in the same places that the live studio audience laughed, give or take a little after-the-fact digital modification. The bell rang and you salivated. (Network executives get very nervous about comedies without the sign-posting of a computer-generated laugh track, which is why such shows are rare. "I come from a place where getting a laugh from an audience is a rather sacred and holy thing," said writer Aaron Sorkin, while trying to sell reluctant ABC brass on a laugh-trackless format for his new show called *Sports Night*. "To make one up by pushing a button on a computer bothers me in a place I don't like to be bothered.")

Zap.

It's Friday night and you're watching that old classic *Risky Business*. A preposterously young-looking Tom Cruise is wearing Ray•Ban Wayfarers, just like yours. Is this a coincidence? The movie came out around about the time your sense of cool was embryonic. You don't remember making a conscious choice about eyewear. The fact is, though, that when it came time to buy sunglasses, you chose Ray•Ban. And you still wear them and you still think they're sharp. So you begin to wonder about this product-placement thing. Just how many other commodity signs are slipping into the Hollywood image stream and influencing your purchasing decisions? The laptop computer you picked up last year. Isn't that the one they used to save the world in *Independence Day*? The Dr Pepper you just bought on impulse. Didn't Forrest Gump drink that stuff?

It used to be jarring to see an actor reach for a Heineken or bring home a tub of Baskin-Robbins ice cream. It meant that reality was intruding on the generic dream world, and it broke the spell. But product placements are everywhere in movies now. (Most people peg the birth of product placement as a full-blown trend to the trail of Reese's Pieces the little alien laid down in *E.T.*, in 1982.) Yet because they're everywhere, they're nowhere. You don't really notice them. Just as you probably don't notice brand names in novels or songs. All fictions grounded in the facts of our life are an easier sell. We'll believe a character who drinks Miller before we'll believe a character who drinks "beer."

What this means is that we're now ripe for manipulation. We can be buzzed by logos without noticing. This is not so different from being buzzed by a laugh track. We've backgrounded these things and—at least consciously—tuned them out. We've given up mental control. To whom? To the dozens of entertainment marketing agencies in the U.S. that specialize in moving products into (and out of!) scripts before movies are ever shot. They act as middlemen between culture and commerce. They spin like lathes behind the scenes so that you don't even think to ask why, for instance, there was only one reference to Nike in *Jerry Maguire*—a movie shot through with the Nike ethos of athlete commodification. (The answer: because Reebok paid Tristar Pictures a million and a half bucks for merchandising, advertising and promotion of *its* product.)

Some companies pay for placement, others don't. So you don't know if the Coke in the frame just happens to be there or if someone paid $100,000 to put it there. You don't know how to distinguish between the story narrative and the corporate-cultural narrative. What does it mean when you don't know? What does it do to your cultural gyrostabilizers, your sense of where, and who, you are?

Zap.

It's August 31, 1997. You catch the breaking news about the death of Princess Diana. Frankly, you couldn't care less about the monarchy, but there was something about plucky Di's style that you liked. You follow the saturation TV coverage: the aftermath, the analysis, the condolences, the funeral. Elton John sings a lachrymose tune and you find yourself weeping in front of your set. It's the middle of the night. The "people's princess" is dead.

Something very odd is happening. You're crying, but you can't locate the source of your tears. It occurs to you that you cried less when some real people you knew—friends and even family members—died. And yet you're crying now. It's crazy. And you're not alone. The global "grieving" for Diana borders on mass hysteria. A lot of people, pressed to articulate *why* they're so sad, admit they're not sad for Di so much as they're sad for the idea of being genuinely sad for someone like her—in the way that teenagers will sometimes admit to being in love with being in love.

In death Princess Di has become a legend. More than that, she has become a cultural signifier, like the swoosh or the Golden Arches. She has what French new-wave philosopher Jean Baudrillard called "commodity sign value." Her face became paired in our minds with all the good things: compassion, humility, philanthropy, love. She had become the quintessential heroine of our culture, what we all wanted to be. For fifteen years, she dressed herself for the media and sold herself publicly, flirting with the camera (even as she claimed to despise the photographers), and for fifteen years we consumed her. She created the unforgettable media moments that primed the tears we cried in front of the TV set. When we bought Di, we bought the brand, not the product.

Zap.

Take stock of your life. Look around at what you drive, wear, eat, smoke, read. Are these things *you*? Would an anthropologist, given a pile of all your material possessions, be able to assemble an accurate portrait of your personality? Would that portrait reflect a true original or a "type"? That laugh you laughed while watching the basketball player get nutted, and those tears you cried for Diana, were they real? Were they authentic?

If they weren't, you may find yourself wondering: What else about me isn't authentic? Do I really like diamonds? Do I find my partner attractive? Do I actually prefer single-malt scotch? Why am I scared to travel to Egypt? Are the myriad daily choices I make, apparently freely, truly the product of my own will?

Richard Condon's 1959 novel, *The Manchurian Candidate*—which was turned into a movie Pauline Kael called "the most sophisticated political satire ever to come out of Hollywood"—tells the story of an American soldier who is captured during the Korean War, shipped to Manchuria and groomed, via brainwashing, to become a robotic assassin programmed to kill the U.S. president upon a predetermined verbal command.

The subtext of the movie is that Americans are being depatterned by propaganda systems they may not understand or even be aware of. The modern consumer is indeed a Manchurian Candidate living in a trance. He has a vague notion that at some point early in his life, experiments were carried out on him, but he can't remember much about them. While he was drugged, or too young to remember, ideas were implanted into his subconscious with a view to changing his behavior. The Manchurian Consumer has been programmed not to kill the president, but to go out and purchase things on one of a number of predetermined commands.

Slogans now come easily to his lips. He has warm feelings toward many products. Even his most innate drives and emotions trigger immediate connections with consumer goods. Hunger equals Big Mac. Drowsiness equals Starbucks. Depression equals Prozac.

And what about that burning anxiety, that deep, almost forgotten feeling of alarm at his lost independence and sense of self? To the Manchurian Consumer, that's the signal to turn on the TV.

POSTHUMAN

I know a young man who has spent the last few years surfing the electronic media. His whole existence has become a surfin' safari. Nothing is more or less important than anything else. He's supernatural now. He picks up a book, skims a sentence. Looks at a bit of this and a bit of that. He absorbs everything, but not deeply. Everything is nonlinear. Nothing can be sustained—not his interest in his job or his colleagues, not even his marriage: If it's not going well, his first instinct is to surf away.

In related news, a colleague recently watched his upstairs neighbor undergo a slow personality shift. It began when she discovered a particular chat group on the Internet. Her mild curiosity about this new world grew into a full-fledged addiction. Day and night she jumped in and out of conversations with strangers on one topic or another. These strangers, who may or may not use their real names or genders, who may or may not tell the truth, came to seem almost like friends. She knew some of them as if they were family.

She lost ten pounds after discovering this chat group—because she forgot to eat. "Sometimes I go out," she'd say, but she didn't mean "out" out, she meant "out" of that chat group and into another site somewhere else on the Net. She was reluctant to sleep because she might miss an interesting thread. One time my friend saw her on the street, and she hadn't showered in four days.

Now she's a very smart woman, but her addiction—she calls it that herself—changed her. She grew so accustomed to typing her thoughts that her verbal skills suffered. She spoke too quickly, running her words together so that it all sounded like one long word. Her eyes were fixed and liquid and her teeth were a strange color. She behaved erratically. She vacuumed at all hours. At one point she considered getting another e-mail address under another name, so she could "flame" herself.

A psychologist might diagnose this woman as being in the early stages of some dissociative disorder. But she's still fairly grounded compared to others who have more fully immersed themselves in cyberculture.

All across the Net, people (mostly young men) haunt cyberhangouts called MUDs (Multiple-User Domains), where role-playing fantasy games are always in progress. These places are as complex and esoteric as the imaginations of the players allow. They are "transformative," in that they let the user determine the outcome.

In her book *Life on the Screen*, American psychoanalyst Sherry Turkle describes one young man, an inveterate webcrawler, who's a character in six MUDs at the same time. In each MUD he is a different person: a teenage girl, a history professor, a dog, an Arthurian knight, a cyborg and William S. Burroughs. In none of them is he actually himself. Yet each persona has come to feel as real to him as his "real" self. When not directly participating in one group, he sometimes puts that self to "sleep." The character is still in the game, can interact with other players on a superficial level via artificial-intelligence programs, and can summon the real guy back to assume his MUD alter ego via a "page" if something exciting is about to happen.

Reading this story about mediated self-constructions reminded me of an article Ann Beattie wrote for *Esquire* about ten years ago. She had tagged along with a bunch of Japanese tourists on a bus ride through San Francisco. What struck her was the way the passengers, confronted with scenes of beauty or recognizable iconography (like the Golden Gate Bridge), reflexively put their cameras to their eyes. Only when these things were thus "framed" did they become valid. Only when they were memorialized on film did they live. This, I think, is the hazardous fallout from an overmediated world, where nothing that happens becomes real until you can make it fit into the spectacle, or make the spectacle fit into it. "I knew a Californian who read his poetry aloud at parties until his friends learned to silence him," writes anthropologist Edmund Carpenter in his book *Oh, What a Blow That Phantom Gave Me!* "But when he played recordings of these same poems, everybody listened." The Situationists might say such tales, as they accumulate, mark the end of authentic experience, and therefore the end of the authentic self.

Perhaps there's no such thing as an authentic self. Maybe Walt Whitman was right: We contain multitudes. Part child, part adult. Androgynes. Cyborgs. We understand intuitively that machines are becoming more like humans, and now via the promise of virtual reality we have the opportunity to meet machines halfway.

The MUD aficionados Sherry Turkle investigates in her books tend to use the Net to create bigger and better (nonauthentic) selves. They often use it to beef up the parts of their lives that are failing in the real, concrete world. In *Life on the Screen*, we meet Matthew, the nineteen-year-old son of a distant, alcoholic dad. In actual life his girlfriend had dumped him, but on the Net his chivalrous MUD persona was enormously attractive to women. Then we meet Gordon, who likewise invests his on-line characters with "qualities he's trying to develop in himself." The game, Turkle concludes, "has heightened his sense of self as a work in progress."

Turkle coins the term "slippages" to refer to "places where persona and self merge, where the multiple personae join to comprise what the individual thinks of as his or her authentic self." MUD addicts end up inhabiting a world somewhere between real life and virtual life. It's too real to be a game, yet too artificial to be real. They hover in "the gap."

To a lesser extent the same could be said of all of us creatures of the media age—which is why a mortal's entry into the world of MUDs seems like a good metaphor for our immersion into what Turkle calls "the culture of simulation." A place where a word like "authenticity" may no longer even apply.

If you spend enough time in cyberspace, emote commands start taking the place of emotions. "Emoticons"—those cunning little sideways faces typed with punctuation marks—substitute for real smiles and frowns. Over time, the computer drives out what we thought was an innate art: living through all of our senses. In her short story "Web Central," Fay Weldon paints a portrait of a dystopic future along these lines: The privileged classes sit alone in sealed rooms with computer terminals, their moods regulated intravenously.

The idea that spending a lot of time in cyberspace might have an ill effect on mental health has until recently been intuitively sensible but hard to prove. In August 1998, findings of the first concentrated study of the social and psychological effects of the Internet, a two-year effort by Carnegie Mellon University, were released. The results? Netheads were lonelier and more depressed than the average population. You'd guess that it might be because the lonely and depressed tend to gravitate to the Net. But that wasn't so. "Participants who were lonelier and more depressed, as determined by standard questionnaires at the start of the . . . study, were no more drawn to the Internet than those who were originally happier and more socially engaged. Instead, Internet use itself appeared to cause a decline in psychological well-being." "Connect, disconnect" may be our generation's answer to "Tune in, turn on, drop out."

Eventually, and perhaps sooner rather than later, there lies a world where most human beings are simply incapable of experiencing the emotions that life ought to evoke. Whatever they see or hear or taste, no matter how raw and beautiful, will promptly be pillaged for its usable constituent parts. And of course, once an emotion is corrupted, it can never be *un*corrupted.

In John Irving's novel *A Prayer for Owen Meany*, the family matriarch dies in front of the television, rigor mortis sets in and her thumb is fixed on the remote. They find her body in front of the live set, the remote endlessly scanning the channels. It's a prophetic image. As we travel deeper into corporate-driven cyberspace, similar haunting figures loom on our own horizon. Fractured humans are laid waste in front of their wall-size TV-cyberscreens. Their attention spans flicker near zero, their imaginations have given out and they can no longer remember the past. Outside, the natural world has all but vanished and the social order is breaking down. The citizens of this new world order are trapped inside their living rooms, roaming the thousand-channel universe and exercising the one freedom they still have left: to be the voyeurs of their own demise.

winter

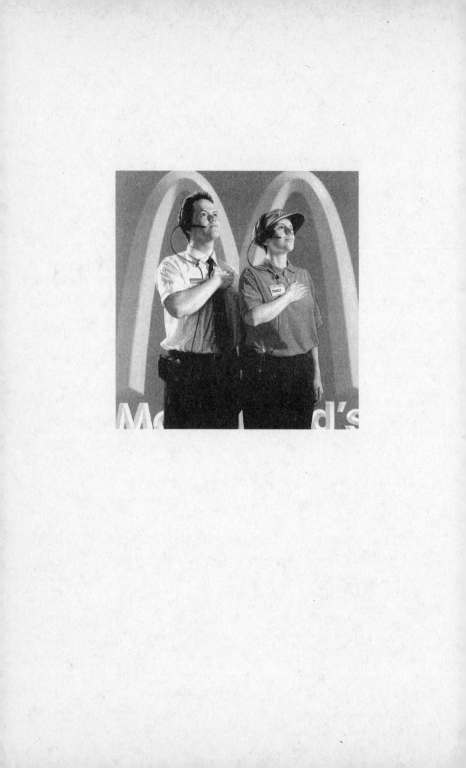

THE CULT YOU'RE IN

A beeping truck, backing up in the alley, jolts you out of a scary dream—a mad midnight chase through a supermarket, ending with a savage beating at the hands of the Keebler elves. You sit up in a cold sweat, heart slamming in your chest. It was only a nightmare. Slowly, you reintegrate, remembering who and where you are. In your bed, in your little apartment, in the very town you grew up in.

It's a "This Is Your Life" moment—a time for mulling and stock-taking. You are still here. Just a few miles from the place you had your first kiss, got your first job (drive-through window at Wendy's), bought your first car ('73 Ford Torino), went nuts with the Wild Turkey on prom night and pulled that all-nighter at Kinko's, photocopying transcripts to send to the big schools back East.

Those big dreams of youth didn't quite pan out. You didn't get into Harvard, didn't get courted by the Bulls, didn't land a recording contract with EMI (or anyone else), didn't make a million by age twenty-five. And so you scaled down your hopes of embarrassing riches to reasonable expectations of adequate comfort—the modest condo downtown, the Visa card, the Braun shaver, the one good Armani suit.

Even this more modest star proved out of reach. The state college you graduated from left you with a $35,000 debt. The work you found hardly dented it: dreadful eight-to-six days in the circulation department of a bad lifestyle magazine. You learned to swallow hard and just do the job—until the cuts came and the junior people were cleared out with a week's severance pay and sober no-look nods from middle management. You began paying the rent with Visa advances. You got call-display to avoid the collection agency.

There remains only one thing no one has taken away, your only real equity. And you intend to enjoy fully that Fiat rustmaster this weekend. You can't run from your problems, but you may as well drive. Road Trip. Three days to forget it all. Three days of living like an animal (in the best possible sense), alert to sights and sounds and smells: Howard Stern on the morning radio, Slumber Lodge pools along the I-14. "You may find yourself behind the wheel of a large automobile," sings David Byrne from a tape labeled "Road Tunes One." The Fiat is, of course, only large at heart. "You know what FIAT stands for?" Liv said when she first saw it. "Fix It Again, Tony." You knew then that this was a girl you could travel to the ends of the Earth with. Or at least to New York City.

The itinerary is set. You will order clam chowder from the Soup Nazi, line up for standby Letterman tickets and wander around Times Square (Now cleaner! Safer!) with one eye on the Jumbotron. It's a place you've never been, though you live there in your mind. You will jog in Battery Park and sip Guinness at Michael's Pub on Monday night (Woody Allen's night), and you will dance with Liv in the Rainbow Room on her birthday. Ah Liv, who when you first saw her spraying Opium on her wrist at the cosmetics counter reminded you so much of Cindy Crawford—though of late she's put on a few pounds and now looks better when you close your eyes and imagine.

And so you'll drive. You'll fuel up with Ho Ho's and Pez and Evian and magazines and batteries for your Discman, and then you'll bury the pedal under your Converse All-Stars—like the ones Kurt Cobain died in. Wayfarers on, needle climbing and the unspoken understanding that you and Liv will conduct the conversation entirely in movie catchphrases.

"Mrs. Nixon would like you to pass the Doritos."

"You just keep thinking, Butch. That's what you're good at."

"It's over, Rock. Nothing on Earth's gonna save you now."

It occurs to you that you can't remember the last time Liv was just Liv and you were just you. You light up a Metro, a designer cigarette so obviously targeted at your demographic . . . which is why you steered clear of them until one day you smoked one to be ironic, and now you can't stop.

You'll come back home in a week. Or maybe you won't. Why should you? What's there to come back *for*? On the other hand, why should you stay?

A long time ago, without even realizing it, just about all of us were recruited into a cult. At some indeterminate moment, maybe when we were feeling particularly adrift or vulnerable, a cult member showed up and made a beautiful presentation. "I believe I have something to ease your pain." She made us feel welcome. We understood she was offering us something to give life meaning. She was wearing Nike sneakers and a Planet Hollywood cap.

Do you *feel* as if you're in a cult? Probably not. The atmosphere is quite un-Moonielike. We're free to roam and recreate. No one seems to be forcing us to do anything we don't want to do. In fact, we feel privileged to be here. The rules don't seem oppressive. But make no mistake: There are rules.

By consensus, cult members speak a kind of corporate Esperanto: words and ideas sucked up from TV and advertising. We wear uniforms—not white robes but, let's say, Tommy Hilfiger jackets or Airwalk sneakers (it depends on our particular subsect). We have been recruited into roles and behavior patterns *we did not consciously choose.*

Quite a few members ended up in the slacker camp. They're bunked in spartan huts on the periphery, well away from the others. There's no mistaking cult slackers for "downshifters"—those folks who have *voluntarily* cashed out of their high-paying jobs and simplified their lives. Slackers are downshifters by necessity. They live frugally because they are poor. (Underemployed and often overeducated, they may never get out of the rent-and-loan-repayment cycle.)

There's really not much for the slackers to *do* from day to day. They hang out, never asking, never telling, just offering intermittent wry observations. They are postpolitical, postreligious. They don't define themselves by who they vote for or pray to (these things are pretty much prescribed in the cult anyway). They set themselves apart in the only way cult members can: by what they choose to wear and drive and listen to. The only things to which they confidently ascribe value are things other people have already scouted, deemed worthy and embraced.

Cult members aren't really citizens. The notions of citizenship and nationhood make little sense in this world. We're not fathers and mothers and brothers: We're consumers. We care about sneakers, music and Jeeps. The only *Life, Freedom, Wonder* and *Joy* in our lives are the brands on our supermarket shelves.

Are we happy? Not really. Cults promise a kind of boundless contentment—punctuated by moments of bliss—but never quite deliver on that promise. They fill the void, but only with a different kind of void. Disillusionment eventually sets in—or it would if we were allowed to think much about it. Hence the first commandment of a cult: *Thou shalt not think.* Free thinking will break the trance and introduce competing perspectives. Which leads to doubt. Which leads to contemplation of the nearest exit.

How did all this happen in the first place? Why have we no memory of it? When were we recruited?

The first solicitations began when we were very young. If you close your eyes and think back, you may remember some of them.

You are four years old, tugging on your mother's sleeve in the supermarket. There are products down here at eye level that she cannot see. Cool products with cartoon faces on them. Toys familiar from Saturday morning television. You want them. She keeps pushing her cart. You cry. She doesn't understand.

You are eight. You have allowance money. You savor the buying experience. A Coke here, a Snickers bar there. Each little fix means not just getting what you want, but *power*. For a few moments *you* are the center of attention. *You* call the shots. People smile and scurry around serving you.

Michael Jordan goes up on your bedroom door. He is your first hero, throwing a glow around the first brand in your life—Nike. You wanna be like Mike.

Other heroes follow. Sometimes they contradict each other. Michael Jackson drinks Pepsi but Michael Jordan drinks Coke. Who is the false prophet? Your friends reinforce the brandhunting. Wearing the same stuff and hearing the same music makes you a fraternity, united in soul and form.

You watch TV. It's your sanctuary. You feel neither loneliness nor solitude here.

You enter the rebel years. You strut the malls, brandishing a Dr Pepper can full of Scotch, which you drink right under the noses of the surveillance guards. One day you act drunk and trick them into "arrest-ing" you—only this time it actually *is* soda in the can. You are immensely pleased with yourself.

You go to college, invest in a Powerbook, ride a Vespa scooter, don Doc Martens. In your town, a new sports complex and performing arts center name themselves after a car manufacturer and a software com-pany. You have moved so far into the consumer maze that you can smell the cheese.

After graduating you begin to make a little money, and it's quite seductive. The more you have, the more you think about it.

You buy a house with three bathrooms. You park your BMW out-side the double garage. When you grow depressed you go shopping.

The cult rituals spread themselves evenly over the calendar: Christ-mas, Super Bowl, Easter, pay-per-view boxing match, summer Olympics, Mother's Day, Father's Day, Thanksgiving, Halloween. Each has its own imperatives—stuff you have to buy, things you have to do.

You're a lifer now. You're locked and loaded. On the go, trying to generate more income to buy more things and then, feeling dissatisfied but not quite sure why, setting your sights on even greater income and

Off

On April 22, people all over the world will turn off their TVs and not turn them on for a week. Why don't you try it? Imagine — no more radiation, laugh tracks or gratuitous violence. It's great! And once you try real life, you may never want to go back to the simulated variety again.

international
tv turnOff week
22-28. April.

escape the fantasy– get real!
www.adbusters.org

more acquisitions. When "consumer confidence is down," spending is "stagnant," the "retail sector" is "hurting" and "stingy consumers are giving stores the blues," you do your bit for the economy. You are a star.

Always, always you have been free to dream. The motivational speakers you watched on late-night TV preached that even the most sorry schleppers can achieve their goals if they visualize daily and stay committed. *Think and grow rich.*

Dreams, by definition, are supposed to be unique and imaginative. Yet the bulk of the population is dreaming the same dream. It's a dream of wealth, power, fame, plenty of sex and exciting recreational opportunities.

What does it mean when a whole culture dreams the same dream?

THE END OF THE AMERICAN DREAM

The past always looks better through the lens of nostalgia. It's human nature to exaggerate how good things once were, how happy everyone was. But in postwar America, things really *were* pretty good. And despite everything we've learned about that era since, people really were fairly happy. A prosperous consumer culture had developed. We bought what we needed, with cash. We tucked away 10 percent of what we earned. We amused ourselves. We read. In summers Mom and Dad took the clan camping on the dunes. This was the American dream: a sprinkler on every lawn, a car in every driveway, a chicken in every pot.

But somewhere along the line, the dream soured. The messages we received grew darker and came faster. The television stayed on all day and the kids logged astonishing hours in front of it. Companies merged and began laying people off. Personal debt grew. People gobbled takeout and started getting fat. Malls, not churches, teemed with families on Sunday mornings. A few critics sounded the alarm that an unencumbered lifestyle of acquisition and consumption would exact its price in the end, but the critics were seen as do-gooders, party poopers, intellectual weenies. Enemies of the American Way.

Now, at the dawn of the third millennium, those early warnings look prophetic. Something has gone terribly wrong. On the surface, life in America is much more stimulating than it was in the '50s. But people are oddly dysphoric. Restless. Unfulfilled. Deadened. Something has happened to us. Something has been taken from us. Our world seems an almost cartoonish distortion of the world we once knew. The family car can't get onto the turnpike for gridlock. The grass is a green not found in nature. Uncle Walter is on a cocktail of pills. Aunt Nellie, aluminum-pot cooking queen, can't remember where she lives. Mom's on Prozac. Mary-Lou's bulimic. Last we heard of Dad he was running a pyramid scheme in Phoenix.

Even in "good" neighborhoods—wealthy neighborhoods, gated neighborhoods, *your* neighborhood—women don't jog alone after dusk. News agencies report that crime rates are falling, but no one feels safer than they did five years ago. In the inner cities, pensioners double-bolt the doors in fear of home invasions, and a trip to the grocery store seems as menacing as a night in the jungle. In some buildings people talk to the other tenants, but mostly they don't, because *why get involved*? Every loner arouses suspicions—was that a power saw you heard in the upstairs apartment?—and there are more loners. The trust that once forged community is almost gone. Who ripped the radio out of your car while you slept last night? Your neighbors shrug; they didn't see or hear a thing. You install The Club and an alarm. Someone smashes the windshield anyway—a political statement, or maybe not. You eventually buy a cheaper car and leave it unlocked. Some mornings you find a street person sleeping in it. On those days you take the bus.

Before leaving for work, sunbelt urbanites tune in to the air-quality report. During inversions, when the smog is trapped over the city, the asthmatic are advised not to venture outside. Bike couriers wear nose-and-mouth masks that make them look vaguely menacing, like Imperial Stormtroopers. The tapwater is rust colored and it smells and tastes, well, industrial. The city says the trace metals are within acceptable limits, but sales of bottled water rise as people play it safe. Then a whole family in California dies from designer water that's been spiked with benzene as a prank. In country after country, studies reveal that men's sperm counts are falling. Nobody quite knows why.

A friend recently recounted a great urban legend. It was about a grand country wedding on the Sunshine Coast of British Columbia. It had been an affair to remember, the union of two well-off and respected families. The reception was held in one of the locals' big, grassy backyards. There was a band, and one by one everyone got up to dance. It turned out that septic pipes ran under that lawn. The weight of dozens of guests bearing down was too much for the system, and the pipes burst. Raw sewage rose up through the grass. It began to cover everyone's shoes. If anybody noticed, they didn't say anything. The champagne flowed, the music continued. Until finally a little boy said, "It smells like shit!" And suddenly everyone realized they were ankle-deep in it.

I think of this story every time I try to explain the creeping dysfunction of North American life. It has happened so gradually that hardly anyone has noticed. Those who *have* clued in apparently figure it's best to ignore the shit and just keep dancing.

In 1945, America was one of history's great liberators. I was a kid in Lübeck, Germany, when the GIs marched in. I still vividly remember their "aw shucks" smiles and the magical way they pulled chewing gum and Hershey bars from their pockets and handed them out to all us kids. My father hailed them as the saviors of the world. Now, fifty years later, America, the great liberator, is in desperate need of being liberated from itself—from its own excesses and arrogance. And the world needs to be liberated from American values and culture, spreading across the planet as if by divine providence.

Yet the American dream is so seductive that most of us willingly keep on dreaming. We continue to drive our cars to the supermarket each week and idly wander the aisles, continue blithely to throw out our weight in trash every few weeks, continue to assume that the additives in our food are harmless shelf-life extenders, continue to play Visa against MasterCard, continue to buy sneakers made in offshore sweatshops, and continue to sit sphinxlike in front of the tube most nights

absorbing another dose of consumer-culture spectacle. The images beckon us to a future in which maximum pleasure and minimum pain are not only possible but inevitable. We yearn to realize the dream more fully. We work and strive for the promised payoff. We try to catch the river in a bucket. But we never will.

We have become what French sociologist Henri Lefebvre called "a bureaucratic society of controlled consumption." Our culture has evolved into a consumer culture and we from citizens to consumers. Gratitude for what we have has been replaced by a sharpening hunger for what we don't have. "How much is enough?" has been replaced by "How much is possible?"

It has not been pretty to watch.

Over a twenty-year period, Elvis Presley evolved from the avatar of American cool to the embodiment of American excess. Almost entirely confined to bed in his last months, Elvis devoured pills and fried-banana-and-peanut-butter sandwiches, suppressing the pain of being Elvis and seemingly trying to lose himself inside his own expanding girth. He was found, appropriately, dead on the throne, head down, like an offensive lineman waiting for the snap. Three points of contact: his fat hands on the tile and his ass on the porcelain.

There is no better metaphor for the old American dream. With a few exceptions, we are all Elvis now. We have learned what it means to live full-on, to fly and fornicate like an American, and now we refuse to let that lifestyle go. So we keep consuming. Our bodies, minds, families, communities, the environment—all are consumed.

THE UNOFFICIAL HISTORY OF AMERICA™

The history of America is the one story every kid knows. It's a story of fierce individualism and heroic personal sacrifice in the service of a dream. A story of early settlers, hungry and cold, carving a home out of the wilderness. Of visionary leaders fighting for democracy and justice, and never wavering. Of a populace prepared to defend those ideals to the death. It's the story of a revolution (an American art form as endemic as baseball or jazz) beating back British imperialism and launching a new colony into the industrial age on its own terms.

It's a story of America triumphant. A story of its rise after World War II to become the richest and most powerful country in the history of the world, "the land of the free and home of the brave," an inspiring model for the whole world to emulate.

That's the official history, the one that is taught in school and the one our media and culture reinforce in myriad ways every day.

The unofficial history of the United States is quite different. It begins the same way—in the revolutionary cauldron of colonial America—but then it takes a turn. A bit player in the official history becomes critically important to the way the unofficial history unfolds. This player turns out to be not only the provocateur of the revolution, but in the end its saboteur. This player lies at the heart of America's defining theme: the difference between a country that pretends to be free and a country that truly is free.

That player is the corporation.

The United States of America was born of a revolt not just against British monarchs and the British parliament but against British corporations.

We tend to think of corporations as fairly recent phenomena, the legacy of the Rockefellers and Carnegies. In fact, the corporate presence in prerevolutionary America was almost as conspicuous as it is today. There were far fewer corporations then, but they were enormously powerful: the Massachusetts Bay Company, the Hudson's Bay Company, the British East India Company. Colonials feared these chartered entities. They recognized the way British kings and their cronies used them as robotic arms to control the affairs of the colonies, to pinch staples from remote breadbaskets and bring them home to the motherland.

The colonials resisted. When the British East India Company imposed duties on its incoming tea (telling the locals they could buy the tea or lump it, because the company had a virtual monopoly on tea distribution in the colonies), radical patriots demonstrated. Colonial merchants agreed not to sell East India Company tea. Many East India Company ships were turned back at port. And, on one fateful day in Boston, 342 chests of tea ended up in the salt chuck.

The Boston Tea Party was one of young America's finest hours. It sparked enormous revolutionary excitement. The people were beginning to understand their own strength, and to see their own self-determination not just as possible but inevitable.

The Declaration of Independence, in 1776, freed Americans not only from Britain but also from the tyranny of British corporations, and for a hundred years after the document's signing, Americans remained deeply suspicious of corporate power. They were careful about the way they granted corporate charters, and about the powers granted therein.

Early American charters were created literally by the people, for the people as a legal convenience. Corporations were "artificial, invisible, intangible," mere financial tools. They were chartered by individual states, not the federal government, which meant they could be kept under close local scrutiny. They were automatically dissolved if they engaged in activities that violated their charter. Limits were placed on how big and powerful companies could become. Even railroad magnate J. P. Morgan, the consummate capitalist, understood that corporations must never become so big that they "inhibit freedom to the point where efficiency [is] endangered."

The two hundred or so corporations that were operating in the U.S. by the year 1800 were each kept on a fairly short leash. They weren't allowed to participate in the political process. They couldn't buy stock in other corporations. And if one of them acted improperly, the consequences were severe. In 1832, President Andrew Jackson vetoed a motion to extend the charter of the corrupt and tyrannical Second Bank of the United States, and was widely applauded for doing so. That same year the state of Pennsylvania revoked the charters of ten banks for operating contrary to the public interest. Even the enormous industry trusts, formed to protect member corporations from external competitors and provide barriers to entry, eventually proved no match for the state. By the mid-1800s, antitrust legislation was widely in place.

In the early history of America, the corporation played an important but subordinate role. The people—not the corporations—were in control. So what happened? How did corporations gain power and eventually start exercising more control than the individuals who created them?

The shift began in the last third of the nineteenth century—the start of a great period of struggle between corporations and civil society. The turning point was the Civil War. Corporations made huge profits from procurement contracts and took advantage of the disorder and corruption of the times to buy legislatures, judges and even presidents. Corporations became the masters and keepers of business. President Abraham Lincoln foresaw terrible trouble. Shortly before his death, he warned, "Corporations have been enthroned. . . . An era of corruption in high places will follow and the money power will endeavor to prolong its reign by working on the prejudices of the people . . . until wealth is aggregated in a few hands . . . and the republic is destroyed."

President Lincoln's warning went unheeded. Corporations continued to gain power and influence. They had the laws governing their creation amended. State charters could no longer be revoked. Corporate profits could no longer be limited. Corporate economic activity could be restrained only by the courts, and in hundreds of cases judges granted corporations minor legal victories, conceding rights and privileges they did not have before.

Then came a legal event that would not be understood for decades (and remains baffling even today), an event that would change the course of American history. In *Santa Clara County* v. *Southern Pacific Railroad*, a dispute over a railbed route, the U.S. Supreme Court deemed that a private corporation was a "natural person" under the U.S. Constitution and therefore entitled to protection under the Bill of Rights. Suddenly, corporations enjoyed all the rights and sovereignty previously enjoyed only by the people, including the right to free speech.

This 1886 decision ostensibly gave corporations the same powers as private citizens. But considering their vast financial resources, corporations thereafter actually had far *more* power than any private citizen. They could defend and exploit their rights and freedoms more vigorously than any individual and therefore they were *more free*. In a single legal stroke, the whole intent of the American Constitution— that all citizens have one vote, and exercise an equal voice in public debates—had been undermined. Sixty years after it was inked, Supreme Court Justice William O. Douglas concluded of *Santa Clara* that it "could not be supported by history, logic or reason." One of the great legal blunders of the nineteenth century changed the whole idea of democratic government.

Post–*Santa Clara* America became a very different place. By 1919, corporations employed more than 80 percent of the workforce and produced most of America's wealth. Corporate trusts had become too powerful to legally challenge. The courts consistently favored their interests. Employees found themselves without recourse if, for example, they were injured on the job (if you worked for a corporation, you voluntarily assumed the risk, was the courts' position). Railroad and mining companies were enabled to annex vast tracts of land at minimal expense.

Gradually, many of the original ideals of the American Revolution were simply quashed. Both during and after the Civil War, America was increasingly being ruled by a coalition of government and business interests. The shift amounted to a kind of coup d'état—not a sudden military takeover but a gradual subversion and takeover of the institutions of state power. Except for a temporary setback during Franklin Roosevelt's New Deal (the 1930s), the U.S. has since been governed as a corporate state.

In the post–World War II era, corporations continued to gain power. They merged, consolidated, restructured and metamorphosed into ever larger and more complex units of resource extraction, production, distribution and marketing, to the point where many of them became economically more powerful than many countries. In 1997, fifty-one of the world's hundred largest economies were corporations, not countries. The top five hundred corporations controlled 42 percent of the world's wealth. Today, corporations freely buy each other's stocks and shares. They lobby legislators and bankroll elections. They manage our broadcast airwaves, set our industrial, economic and cultural agendas, and grow as big and powerful as they damn well please.

Every day, scenes that would have seemed surreal, impossible, undemocratic twenty years ago play out with nary a squeak of dissent from a stunned and inured populace.

At Morain Valley Community College in Palos Hills, Illinois, a student named Jennifer Beatty stages a protest against corporate sponsorship in her school by locking herself to the metal mesh curtains of the multimillion-dollar "McDonald's Student Center" that serves as the physical and nutritional focal point of her college. She is arrested and expelled.

At Greenbrier High School in Evans, Georgia, a student named Mike Cameron wears a Pepsi T-shirt on the day—dubbed "Coke Day"—when corporate flacks from Coca-Cola jet in from Atlanta to visit the school their company has sponsored and subsidized. Mike Cameron is suspended for his insolence.

In suburban shopping malls across North America, moms and dads push shopping carts down the aisle of Toys "R" Us. Trailing them and imitating their gestures, their kids push pint-size carts of their own. The carts say, "Toys 'R' Us Shopper in Training."

In St. Louis, Missouri, chemical giant Monsanto sics its legal team on anyone even considering spreading dirty lies—or dirty truths— about the company. A Fox TV affiliate that has prepared a major investigative story on the use and misuse of synthetic bovine growth hormone (a Monsanto product) pulls the piece after Monsanto attorneys threaten the network with "dire consequences" if the story airs. Later, a planned book on the dangers of genetic agricultural technologies is temporarily shelved after the publisher, fearing a lawsuit from Monsanto, gets cold feet.

In boardrooms in all the major global capitals, CEOs of the world's biggest corporations imagine a world where they are protected by what is effectively their own global charter of rights and freedoms—the Multinational Agreement on Investment (MAI). They are supported in this vision by the World Trade Organization (WTO), the World Bank, the International Monetary Fund (IMF), the International Chamber of Commerce (ICC), the European Round Table of Industrialists (ERT), the Organization for Economic Co-operation and Development (OECD) and other organizations representing twenty-nine of the world's richest economies. The MAI would effectively create a single global economy allowing corporations the unrestricted right to buy, sell and move their businesses, resources and other assets wherever and whenever they want. It's a corporate bill of rights designed to override all "nonconforming" local, state and national laws and regulations and allow them to sue cities, states and national governments for alleged noncompliance. Sold to the world's citizens as inevitable and necessary in an age of free trade, those MAI negotiations met with considerable grassroots opposition and were temporarily suspended in April 1998. Nevertheless, no one believes this initiative will remain suspended for long.

We, the people, have lost control. Corporations, these legal fictions that we ourselves created two centuries ago, now have more rights, freedoms and powers than we do. And we accept this as the normal state of affairs. We go to corporations on our knees. *Please* do the right thing, we plead. *Please* don't cut down any more ancient forests. *Please* don't pollute any more lakes and rivers (but please don't move your factories and jobs offshore either). *Please* don't use pornographic images to sell fashion to my kids. *Please* don't play governments off against each other to get a better deal. We've spent so much time bowed down in deference, we've forgotten how to stand up straight.

The unofficial history of America™, which continues to be written, is not a story of rugged individualism and heroic personal sacrifice in the pursuit of a dream. It is a story of democracy derailed, of a revolutionary spirit suppressed, and of a once-proud people reduced to servitude.

YOUR CORPORATE CONNECTION

Meet Janet, high school valedictorian, devoted daughter, middle-distance track star. The almost perfect kid. But Janet has a secret ritual and she'd like to *keep* it that way. After meals, she routinely excuses herself to the bathroom and shoves two fingers down her throat. A couple of her friends have divined her eating disorder from the clues: She's reed-thin and has a chronic cough. She's on the StairMaster at the Y for an hour a day and two hours on weekends. She's constantly popping breath mints. The stomach acid she brings up is dissolving the enamel on her teeth, which are unnaturally white. The skin on her face seems opalescent, and her eyes shine. She's dying.

Meet Matt and Sarah, already dubbed the perfect couple though they've only known each other three months. Sarah is one of those people who are always getting asked to be a bridesmaid. She's smart, funny, spunky and kind. Matt's family adores her. His friends sometimes call her up just to talk. When's the wedding?

As it turns out, never. Matt has just broken things off. He had to be honest: She was just not cute enough. Whatever sexual spark might have been there on day one—the novelty of a new scent, a new body to explore—is gone. He wishes it hadn't happened. He wishes she still turned him on. But she doesn't.

Sarah is not unattractive, but she's not exactly Elle McPherson either. Ten years of conditioning—slavering over his dad's old *Playboy*s, collecting *Sports Illustrated* swimsuit editions and trolling the porn sites on the Internet—have taught him, at an almost cellular level, that Elle McPherson and her ilk are what desirable women look like. Those little parabolas where the hips flare from a twenty-five-inch waist. The gravity-free breasts. When Matt and Sarah made love, he could only get aroused if he imagined she was Elle, all hair and tan and Australian accent. In time, his imagination failed him. He drew back. "Houston," he actually said to himself one night, watching her breathe in her sleep, "we have a problem."

Meet Randy, bartender and gym rat. At around age nineteen, Randy acquired a suit of armor. It is his own musculature. At work, in a tight white Hugo Boss T-shirt, he looks merely fit. But when he's pumped—which is about three hours out of every day—he swells to almost comic-book proportions. The veins on his arms stand out like rivers. His workout buddies call him "The Big Unit," after Astros closer Randy Johnson. Size matters, but size has proved relative. He has found that building the perfect body is a little like building the perfect stereo system: When you improve one component, everything else becomes underpowered by comparison and must therefore be upgraded. The pecs, the delts, the glutes. Check the mirror for symmetry and shape. Thus is born obsession. Occasional steroid use has shrunk Randy's balls and scarred his face with acne.

Their lives and circumstances are very different, but Janet, Matt, Sarah and Randy all have this in common: They're meat on the killing floor of the body-image factory. The way they think about themselves as physical beings has become grossly distorted. They've lost control of their sexuality. They are no longer making the decisions about how they should look, what they should feel, or what constitutes a successful relationship.

Then who is? There's no single, simple answer to that, but I think it's fair to say a vast network of opinion-shapers is involved. It's not a conspiracy, exactly. The controlling elite are simply people with powerful media access who are all pushing in the same direction. These people work on Madison Avenue and Savile Row, in Hollywood and Paris and Milan. One way or another, their checks are cut by the beauty industry, which has persuaded us that if we are thin and toned and well tailored, we will be loved. They have manipulated us badly.

And they have done it subtly, feeding our insecurities a little at a time.

Fact: Nine out of ten North American women feel bad about some aspect of their bodies, and men are not far behind. A 1992 survey of eleven- to fifteen-year-old Canadian girls revealed that 50 percent thought they should be thinner. They didn't wish they *were* thinner, they thought they *should* be thinner, as if being thin were a kind of cultural law. Now girls as young as five are watching what they eat. If you randomly survey North American women, you'll find that around 50 percent of them are on a diet. If you ask adolescent girls and young women, you'll find that figure around 60 percent. Healthy women are sometimes led by women's magazines or unscrupulous cosmetic surgeons to believe they suffer from such "afflictions" as "violin deformity" (a flaring of the hips, which is in fact many women's natural body shape) or "batwing disorder" (loose skin under the arms, which is quite normal)—and feel compelled to go under the knife to remedy them. Some models have removed their bottom ribs to accentuate the thinness of their waists.

But all this media-fed body consciousness is not just about being thin.

Fact: Half of all exotic dancers were once beauty-pageant contestants. That's a surprising statistic when you first hear it. It's hard to bridge the distance between the wholesome, naive, small-town Cavalcade Queen who plays "The Volga Boatman" on the accordion and wants to be a vet, to the hardened stripper with seen-it-all eyes grinding in red light on the stage of Number Five Orange. However, the more you think about it, the more sense it makes. From the instant the twelve-year-old pageant contestant (and some pageant queens are groomed much younger than this, as JonBenet Ramsey proved) steps in front of a crowd, a kind of tractor beam takes hold of her. She feels the electricity of what anthropologists sometimes call "the male gaze." She understands that the sum of her worth, at that moment, to these people, lies in the image she presents. The men study her lipstick, complexion, hair, legs and budding breasts. She becomes acutely self-conscious. She's either seduced by or a little terrified of the attention. Or both. Appearance has never been more important and within her latent sexuality (or at least her cultivated seductiveness) lies incredible power—power that, ten years later, she may discover can be parlayed into a pretty fair living on a peeler-bar stage. For maybe five or ten years. For as powerful as the male gaze is, it's also fickle. When it shuts down, the heat leaves the room pretty quickly.

This isn't a terribly original point to make. But I think the fact that it's now almost a cliché—objectification distorts a person's sense of worth—is a dangerous development. We think we understand the paradigm, but I don't believe we do. I don't think many of us have really let its seriousness, its implications sink in. We don't understand what's at stake.

What does it mean that so many of us are willing to give up so much of our power, voluntarily, systematically, to strangers? What does it mean that we're willing to barter the most private parts of ourselves—our way of thinking about ourselves, our way of being in the world—for a brief buzz of attention?

I don't think we have a clear idea of what's going on. Maybe we don't want to know. Perpetually children at some level, we give ourselves up to the reassuringly strong hands of Calvin Klein and Estée Lauder and Donna Karan. We follow their lead. We let them seduce us and possess us, and from our relationship with them we derive a certain sense of security, the way prostitutes derive a sense of security from their pimps. This becomes the implicit contract: *You work for me (i.e., you wear my clothes and makeup) and I will guard your place in the social hierarchy. I will protect your turf. Without me, you know you would not*

feel safe going out. I ensure that you are not hurt out there, and for that you owe me. For me you will try harder, you will look your best; no matter how weak you feel, how broken, you will keep going out there each day because you know that only I can give you the fix you need.

To a large extent, out there in the social world, we find that the beauty industry has engineered our concept of what a good relationship and good sex are all about. It has reinforced a rather odd way of keeping our insecurities in check.

"You can always tell a couple who are on a first date," says a friend who worked as a waitress in a dessert café in Vancouver. "She's not eating. He's got a big slab of cake but she's not eating. Just to be social she might nibble a bite or two from his plate, with her own fork, but she won't order her own dessert. It's not so much that she's worried about looking like a pig if she eats. It's that eating anything makes her *feel* like a pig. And when a girl starts feeling like a pig it's very easy to convince herself that she is. She's a pig. No one—not this guy, not any guy—will ever find her attractive ever again."

A day in your life.

8 A.M.: You are biting into a hash brown patty at McDonald's. The grease shines on your chin like baby oil. You are reminded of your childhood.

What you don't know: One out of every four restaurant-prepared breakfasts in the U.S. is eaten at McDonald's. Every three hours a new McDonald's opens somewhere in the world. The company spends over $1 billion every year on advertising.

9:30 A.M.: You are pushing a cart down the aisle of your neighborhood supermarket, past little pyramids of shiny apples and peppers. You buy Brussels sprouts as well as cocoa, sugar, coffee and bananas. You marvel at a food system that can deliver asparagus in February. You toss a nice ripe, red tomato into the basket.

What you don't know: These vegetables were pumped full of chemicals to enable them to grow in poor soil and survive the voyage to market. The apples and peppers shine because of thick, petroleum-based waxes. The nice ripe, red tomato, a "Flavr Savr," is genetically speaking part flounder. (The technology for this process is owned by chemical giant Monsanto.) A UCLA study of supermarket Brussels sprouts found almost no trace of vitamins in them. "Cash crops" like cocoa, sugar, coffee and bananas—generally grown to supply the First World—pull more and more land away from traditional food crops and fail to protect the soil, often leading to famine. The food you eat comes from wherever it can be grown most cheaply.

6:00 P.M.: The frozen dinner you're about to heat up in the microwave looks virtually the same as the meal you had on the airplane last night.

What you don't know: Boeing, which built that airplane you flew on last night, had to widen its seats in the 1970s because its passengers had grown too fat to fit them. Airline-style food is a good example of the kind of food Americans favor: processed, convenient, leached of nutrients but high in fat. The United States is the fattest nation on Earth and getting fatter. Americans consume more calories per capita, more snacks between meals and more sugar-rich sodas than anyone else. Fat makes up almost 40 percent of all the calories we consume.

9:00 P.M. Evening snack of diet Coke (you're watching calories).

What you don't know: Flight attendants sometimes use diet Coke to unclog sinks in commercial jets.

Eating is a complex act. It's loaded with moral, psychological, social and sexual freight. To say food is simply fuel is like saying marriage is simply a rent-sharing agreement. Food is sin. It's guilt. It's joy. We overeat, then we undereat.

We *want* to listen to our bodies, but Frito-Lay has jammed our feedback mechanisms. We want to eat a naturally healthy diet, but the world's largest suppliers of processed foods have taught us to trust convenience, comfort and the taste of sugar, fat and salt. We've lost the sacred joy of the feast.

In the movie *Babette's Feast*, a French housekeeper uses her lottery winnings to prepare one amazing meal for the puritanical residents of a Norwegian island. For them, the meal is excessively, almost pornographically, sensuous. They have become so accustomed to not deriving pleasure from their meals that they cannot accept this gift from Babette. Many of us raised on processed-food diets are like those islanders. Real, flavorful, sensuous food is so foreign to us we don't know how to respond to it anymore. We've lost our ability to appreciate it. We'd just as soon eat something packaged.

Gone the evening meal, once a joyous ritual of family life. Gone the prayerful acknowledgment of the harvest. Gone the connection between the actual growing of food and its consumption.

Losing this connection is a little like losing a great old friend. The old friend played many roles and enriched our life in many unexpected ways. But over time she grew distant. We allowed outside parties— processors, shippers, factory farmers, supermarketers, junk food merchants—to come between us. By buying into an industrialized food system, we have, as it were, traded in our great old friend for new friends: food brands and corporate buddies.

These new friends are very attentive. McDonald's is never more than about fifteen minutes away. A chocolate fix is as close as the nearest 7-Eleven. The local supermarket now does much of the cooking for us. Monsanto has taken on the job of planning our biotech future.

More and more, our relationship with the industrial food industry begins to resemble the one it has with its chickens, pigs and cows. In exchange for zero responsibility, we get zero control. Soon freedom is just a vestigial memory. We cannot imagine ever having lived differently.

"It's the most bizarre thing," a journalist friend said one recent Monday. Her nose and cheeks were flushed. She looked younger somehow. She seemed scattered, blissed out. She'd clearly spent a scandalous weekend. Was it love?

Yes, she admitted, it was.

"I'm in love with my car."

A week earlier she'd bought a new Jeep, and she'd spent the last couple of days roaring around with the top down, getting a sunburn.

The impression was that of a woman who suddenly discovers, after twenty years of driving a VW van, that life is not about practicality—it's about fun. She grinned for no reason, thinking of that car, remembering the way it smelled and handled corners, remembering it was *hers*. She was looking forward to bonding with new members of the four-by-four tribe: swapping waxing tips and exchanging two-finger waves at stoplights. On special occasions, or as a reward for a good report card, she'd let her daughter drive it to school. She was an "it" mom now and she knew it. She felt it.

I understood. People have intense, sometimes obsessive relationships with their cars. If you own one, think about how much time you spend nurturing the bond. Think of all the hours you spend cleaning it, changing its oil, hunting it down in parking lots, waiting for it at the mechanic's and renewing its insurance. (Not to mention the hours you spend alone together on the road.)

In the movie *Swingers,* any guy with an uncool car—or worse, no car at all—is immediately "Shaqed" (rejected) by any woman he meets. Cars are identifiers. They complete us, they renew us, they reinvent us. Which explains why so many of us dutifully walk into a car showroom every few years for a rejuvenating boost.

Cars are about time—about creating more of it. Instant mobility! (Of course, when you stop to do the math you realize that's not quite true. In most medium-size cities you can get to most places faster by bicycle than by car.)

Cars are about speed—the illusion of pulling astronaut-caliber Gs, even if you're just cornering a little too quickly on the way to the laundromat.

They're about trust—that moment when Dad silently hands over the keys, for the first time, to his eighteen-year-old son. (*Have a good time. Please don't wrap yourself around a telephone pole.*)

I run around in a 1987 Toyota. The last time I changed the oil I noticed that the bolt holding the oil pan on was stripped and oil was leaking out. I went to my authorized Toyota dealer and had to cough up $7 for that little bolt. The guy behind the counter openly admitted it was a rip-off. "But where else are you gonna go?" He laughed. That kind of gouging, which over the years has become normal practice throughout the auto industry, long ago soured my relationship with the automakers.

I don't like the planned obsolescence, which has also become normal practice. Cars aren't like computers: They don't become grossly underequipped for the job every few years. Yet the models change dramatically year after year. Around year two or three, little things start to break down or wear out, and somehow we become convinced that trading in the old bomb for a brand-new model is the smart thing to do.

I don't like the way cars, over the last half century, have eroded our sense of village and the vitality of our neighborhoods. "Once trucks can move produce into your area 24 hours a day, local produce markets disappear," notes Jane Holtz Kay in *Asphalt Nation*. "Once ambulances can get to your place on the freeway, doctors stop making housecalls. The arteries may be alive, but the beating heart of community is hard to find."

I don't like the way the global automakers, with their billion-dollar marketing budgets and their unchallenged fifty-year run on television, have kept the personal automobile—arguably the most destructive product we humans have ever produced—at the center of our transportation agendas for so long.

I don't like the fact that the price of cars does not tell the ecological truth and that the environmental costs of driving are blithely passed on to future generations to the tune of hundreds of billions of dollars every year.

Most of all I don't like the way the global automakers and oil companies minimize and sidestep these issues—how, instead of facing the problems of global warming and climate change head on, they deliberately obfuscate with lyrical advertising campaigns that promote the preposterous idea that their industry is eco-friendly.

I hate all these things and yet I still drive my Toyota. The love of convenience, the time I save, the speed and the power, and the lack of viable alternatives trump my hate more often than not. And so my relationship with my Toyota and the auto industry is full of guilt and angst and barely repressed anger. It's the same kind of slow burn that busts up marriages, twenty-five years down the road, with a violently cathartic act involving an ax or an attorney.

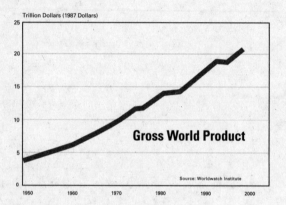

Trillion Dollars (1987 Dollars)

Gross World Product

Source: Worldwatch Institute

THE GLOBAL ECONOMIC PYRAMID SCHEME

Seven men with genial smiles stand shoulder to shoulder on a broad lawn inside a matrix of cordoned-off boulevards. A hundred photographers snap their picture. The seven call each other by their first names, but just about everyone else calls them "Mister." The police are on high alert. The G-7 economic summit is one of the very few occasions where the leaders of the most affluent nations are together in one place. If aliens were planning an effective tactical strike on Earth, here and now would be the best time and place.

These seven men, here to coordinate their economic, financial and trade policies, stand at the helm of the global economy. Between them they control more than two thirds of the world's wealth. They carry the clout within the World Bank and the International Monetary Fund. They wield the power at the World Trade Organization. When their finance ministers say "Go" by lowering taxes and interest rates, people around the world open their wallets. When they say "Stop" by pulling the macroeconomic levers the other way, people grow nervous. They cut back. Jobs are lost. Lives are put on hold.

Of course, the global economy is like the gorilla that sits where it wants; the G-7 leaders don't have a firm rein on it. However, through their power to direct global economic policies, and through reassuring spectacles like the G-7 summit, the leaders create the *perception* of mastery. And in politics, perception is everything. The leaders maintain their authority because *we believe.*

At every summit the focal point of discussion is how to maintain economic growth. Growth is the sine qua non of consumer capitalism. Without growth the global economy as it is currently structured makes no sense. There seem to be no alternatives. But there *is* an alternative—one that has never been discussed at any summit.

Two Schools of Thought

The view that in good times or bad, growth will set us free is a classic argument coming from economics' so-called expansionist camp. Expansionism remains the dominant economic paradigm because expansionists (sometimes called neoclassical economists) are the dominant economic policymakers of our time. They are the professors at our universities, the policy advisers to our governments, the brains in most of the think tanks. Their confident logic shapes the economic strategies by which we live.

The competing view of global economic reality—the ecological worldview—is the new kid on the block. Its vision is not quite fully formed, its logic is a little less confident. Its proponents probably make up fewer than one in fifty of all the practicing economists and economics professors in the world today. Though rapidly growing in acceptance, ecological economics has so far been little more than a minor irritant to its dominant expansionist rival.

The two worldviews are chalk and cheese. Or, if you like, heaven and hell.

Ecological economists (also known as bioeconomists) foresee an apocalypse. They warn that we have reached a unique juncture in human history—that, ecologically speaking, the world is already "full" and further expansion will lead us into an ecological nightmare, a prolonged and possibly permanent "age of despair."

The expansionists, by contrast, see growth not as a problem but as the solution to our economic woes. There is no reason why growth cannot continue indefinitely, they claim. "There are no . . . limits to the carrying capacity of the Earth that are likely to bind at any time in the foreseeable future," pronounced Lawrence Summers, former chief economist of the World Bank. "There isn't a risk of an apocalypse due to global warming or anything else. The idea that the world is headed over an abyss is profoundly wrong. The idea that we should put limits on growth because of some natural limit is a profound error."

This almost unbelievably arrogant view is shared by other expansionists who put their faith in technology. "If it is easy to substitute other factors for natural resources," says Nobel laureate Robert Solow, "then . . . the world can, in effect, get along without natural resources, so exhaustion is just an event, not a catastrophe." The late Julian Simon, author of *Scarcity or Abundance? A Debate on the Environment*, once boasted: "We have in our hands—in our libraries really—the technology to feed, clothe, and supply energy to an ever-growing population for the next seven billion years."

Within the ecological camp, of course, these are fighting words. Worse, they're grievously irresponsible and just plain false. William Rees, coauthor of *Our Ecological Footprint* and a leading spokesman of the new economics, warns that the fivefold expansion in world economic activity since World War II (and a twentyfold increase this century) "has produced an unprecedented level of material and energy exchange between the ecosphere and the human economic subsystem." He points out that 40 percent of terrestrial and 25 percent of marine photosynthesis have now been diverted to human use. He sees ozone depletion, climate change, deforestation, soil degradation and the loss of biodiversity as unambiguous warning signals telling us to stop stressing our ecosphere or die. In 1994, fifty-eight World Academy of Science directors released a document declaring, essentially, that humankind is proceeding down an unprecedented and catastrophic path which will destroy the support systems upon which life depends. Overpopulation, overconsumption, inappropriate technological applications and economic expansion are changing the biophysical features of the Earth.

Ecological economists accuse expansionists of pawning the family silverware—of "liquidating" the planet's irreplaceable natural capital for short-term gain. Robert Ayres, in the *Journal of the International Society for Ecological Economics*, writes: " . . . there is every indication that human economic activity, supported by perverse trade and 'growth' policies, is well on the way to perturbing our natural environment more, and faster, than any known event in planetary history, save perhaps the large asteroid collision that may have killed off the dinosaurs. We humans may well be on the way to our own extinction."

Ecological Economics

Assume for a moment that our survival is indeed threatened. What do we do? How can we address that threat? An obvious answer is to pursue sustainability. To design a new economic system that gives us what we need without sacrificing the well-being of future generations. For ecological economists (or bioeconomists), leveling the playing field between generations is *the* big challenge of our time. Nothing else comes close. And the solution is nothing short of a cultural revolution—an about-face in our values, lifestyles and institutional agendas. A reinvention of the American dream.

Expansionists see the pursuit of sustainability as a much simpler proposition: Create as much wealth as possible by freeing up markets, privatizing government services and eliminating barriers to trade. This will, according to their theories, produce a new round of economic expansion that will create the wealth we need to tackle environmental degradation, poverty and other economic woes.

But there's a flaw in the expansionists' argument. They have no accurate way of measuring the economic progress they keep talking about. Their only measure of growth is the Gross Domestic Product (GDP), and it is seriously flawed.

Consider: When the *Exxon Valdez* spilled its load of oil onto the

Alaskan coast, $2 billion was spent trying to clean up and minimize the ecological damage. That money then circulated throughout the American economy, resulting in a significant increase in the GDP. When the Gulf War broke out, America's GDP rose again. Money changed hands. The country became "healthier." Indeed, every time there's a car accident or a newly diagnosed cancer patient, whenever personal or societal catastrophes occur, the GDP goes up and the economy "gains."

Consider: Walking, biking and using mass transit contribute less to the GDP than using a car. Trains contribute less than airplanes; an extra blanket or sweater contributes less than raising the thermostat; one-child families contribute less than six-child families; eating potatoes contributes less than eating beef; starting a vegetable garden contributes less than buying produce at the supermarket; staying home to raise your daughter contributes less than getting a part-time job at Wendy's. Indeed, the GDP fails to assign any value at all to unpaid or volunteer work. Work done by tens of millions of North Americans simply does not show up on the expansionists' radar. Similarly, the GDP fails to assign any value to declining fish stocks or disappearing forests. It's as if these negatives simply don't exist.

The GDP measures "goods" but not "bads." It cannot distinguish economic benefit for social gain from economic benefit for social loss. Conducting economic policy based solely on the GDP, says Canadian political scientist Ronald Coleman, is like driving your car without a gas gauge. The engine seems to be running fine, but for how long? There's no way to know.

That's why ecological economists have spurned the GDP and developed their own measures of economic progress. The three graphs on page 91 show the GDPs of the U.S., U.K. and Germany all soaring merrily upward from 1955 through the 1980s. However, a more accurate measure of economic progress, the ISEW (Index of Sustainable Economic Welfare), developed by Herman Daly and John Cobb in 1990, tells another story. When some of the "bads," such as pollution, depletion of nonrenewable resources and car exhaust–related health costs, are factored in, a very different picture of the economy emerges.

The U.S., German and U.K. economies all show no improvement in economic welfare since the 1970s. In fact, economic welfare levels off and starts falling quite dramatically in each country.

The ISEW (as well as the GPI, or Genuine Progress Indicator, pioneered by the San Francisco think tank Redefining Progress) exposes the expansionists as a bunch of eager beavers without a well-considered business plan, pseudoscientists urging the world to follow their lead before they themselves have clear bearings. Neoclassical economists cling to their mathematical models like children to their teddy bears. They operate in a kind of academic isolation that does not acknowledge the effects of their policies on the real world. Their world is the world of "revealed preferences" and "rational expectations," of "perfectly voluntary exchange" and "negative externalities" that can be dismissed. Their world is not our world. Their world does not exist.

"The difference between science and economics," says Ferdinand Banks in *Truth and Economics*, "is that science aims at an understanding of the behavior of nature, while economics is involved with an understanding of models—and many of these models have no relation to any state of nature that has ever existed on this planet, or any that is likely to exist between now and doomsday. The word that comes to mind when confronted by these fantasies is fraud."

The Doomsday Machine

In 1996, news stories of a bizarre and tragic wholesale fraud began filtering out of Eastern Europe. In Bulgaria, Romania, Russia, Serbia and Albania, citizens who had sunk their savings into investment schemes that promised money for nothing got a glimpse of the dark side of the free market. In Albania close to 90 percent of the dirt-poor population had put some or all of its money in "foundations," which were actually simple pyramid schemes. No one knew what they were investing in, exactly, but the pitches were electrifying, the promised returns too enticing to resist: cars, tropical vacations, triple your money in three months, a new and better life for everyone. The people believed. And

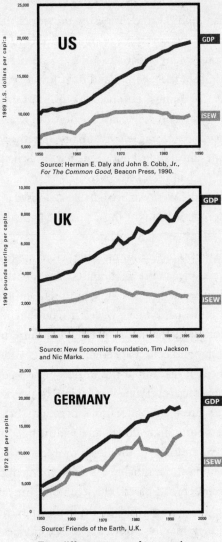

Source: Herman E. Daly and John B. Cobb, Jr.,
For The Common Good, Beacon Press, 1990.

Source: New Economics Foundation, Tim Jackson
and Nic Marks.

Source: Friends of the Earth, U.K.

Two different ways of measuring
economic progress: Gross Domestic
Product (GDP) and the Index of Sustainable Economic Welfare (ISEW). When
pollution, depletion of nonrenewable
resources, car exhaust–related health
costs and other social and ecological
costs are subtracted from the GDP, then
economic "progress" levels off around
1975 and starts falling thereafter.

why not? "Albanian money is the cleanest in the world," reassured President Sali Berisha. If the government endorsed these schemes, surely they were legitimate. Many Albanians took the plunge. They bet the family fruit stands, sold their homes and their livestock. In Albania, as elsewhere in post-Communist Europe, new investors eventually dried up and the funds began failing. Finally, the house of cards came down. People rioted. They had nothing left. Albanians collectively lost a billion dollars—three times the national budget deficit. They had trusted their government and they had been betrayed.

The response in the West was predictable. Bemused pity might best sum it up. We shook our heads at those poor benighted bastards who had been persuaded to "bet on miracles."

But how different is *our* economic fable? Don't we trust our financial advisers, our expansionist economists, our political leaders as blindly as Albanians trusted theirs? Most of us have no idea where our money is. It's not in the bank where we left it. The bank injected it into the bloodstream of the global money market. Vast sums move through this market every day and collect at certain hot spots. After a Canadian company announced it had found the world's biggest gold deposit in the Indonesian rain forest, everyone wanted in. The penny stock soared to nearly $300 a share—until allegations of fraud surfaced and the house of cards came tumbling down, and with it billions of investor dollars, including hundreds of millions invested through pension funds. We sink billions into mutual funds and retirement plans, assuming these to be secure, broad-based, blue-chip investments. But what's in these funds? Just as with hot dogs, you don't really want to know. Some of your money may be bolstering the economies of dubious, often atrocious, even genocidal regimes.

About half a million people around the world wake up every day, leave the world of people, work and nature, and play money games in cyberspace. They invent new instruments (futures, bonds, derivatives, arbitrage, etc.), each with its own risks and rewards, creating $50 in play money for every $1 worth of real products and services actually circulating in the world. They further inflate the amount of "money" in the system by borrowing from each other and bidding up prices. Trillions of dollars slosh around this system every day making billions of dollars of virtual profits for the nimble and the quick. Even as these people sleep, their computers continue searching for margins of profit, automatically triggering buys and sell-offs when the conditions are right.

At the U.S. investment house Kidder Peabody, a single trader reports $1.7 trillion in phony trades over two years before he is caught. At Barings Bank in Britain a young broker, praised for having an "almost unique capacity" to produce big profits without taking significant risks, loses $1.3 billion in one month. He bankrupts the 233-year-old bank with his enthusiasm for Japanese futures.

Those famed, highly speculative "derivatives" aren't just the special currency of young sharks. The accounting firm of Ernst and Young revealed in 1997 that nearly a third of the investment funds it had been tracking included derivatives. Overall, 97 percent of the world's monetary transactions are now speculative. In 1970, the figure hovered around 30 percent.

Blind trust is a scary thing. We give up control of our money. We assume the markets will hold and our nest eggs will grow, when in truth our investment portfolio is often held together with baling wire and blind faith.

And what about the global economy? Is it viable? Is there enough real "estate," real factories, real jobs, real gold mines? Is there enough good topsoil? Are there enough fish left in the sea? Is there enough real economic progress to keep the whole thing growing? And if so, for how long?

On October 27, 1987—Black Monday—the Dow Jones Industrial Average fell 554 points, the biggest single-day plunge in ten years. Circuit breakers on the NYSE kicked in and shut down trading. Just days earlier, Hong Kong's Hang Seng Index had suffered a similar crash, joining a half dozen Asian economies that had fallen or would soon fall in a domino effect of pessimism. Americans—a plucky lot—rebounded quickly. Analysts here called the dive a "correction." Investors jumped back in and the Dow was soon soaring toward 10,000 again, as if nothing had happened. But something *had* happened. The synchronized crashes showed the awesome degree to which world markets are now codependent; how the global economy is now one entity. Everything we do has global implications. Crisis is never far away. The Japanese, Chinese and Asian "tiger" economies have proven much more precarious than we thought. Our own economy depends, to a great extent, on managed public moods and panic held at bay by carefully scripted reassurances from the G-7 leaders and Alan Greenspan at the U.S. Federal Reserve. What would happen if, on top of our current insecurities, the fear of escalating climate change (planetary ecology and economy caught in a deadly downward spiral) suddenly became real to us? Here's a good guess: a crash to dwarf Black Friday and Black Monday. You've got to wonder how long we can continue playing the neoclassical expansionist game, living off our natural capital and calling it income, before the pyramid collapses and the G-7 leaders head for the hills.

The Albanians may have been naive, but their actions were understandable. They had to do *something* with their money because it was rapidly losing its worth. The Japanese, Koreans, Malaysians, Indonesians, and to some degree the rest of us are now caught in a similar vise. We're worried about the future. We don't want to suffer in our old age. We want a secure sum to retire on. We're nervous and impatient. We want our money to grow quickly. So we try stocks, bonds and futures, and hope our nest egg is growing. "Invest my money wisely," we tell our brokers and we place our future in their hands.

Pyramid schemes depend on a continuous supply of dupes (early contributors being paid from the pockets of later ones). When no new contributors can be found, these schemes fail. In the expansionist model of the global economy, future generations—our children and our children's children—are the dupes. As supplies of clean water and air grow scarce, as forests, cod, salmon and wildlife vanish, as climatic instability escalates, we will eventually reach a point where one generation suddenly balks, unable to buy into the scheme. How close we are to that moment of truth is anybody's guess.

Recently I saw a TV news item about a town in Nebraska where the accumulating smoke from wood-burning stoves was making the residents sick. Asthma sufferers had to be hospitalized. Children couldn't play outside after school. A local bylaw was finally enacted to restrict wood burning to Monday, Wednesday and Friday afternoons. Many townspeople were outraged. How dare someone tell me what to do in my own home! they howled. What's next? You're going to tell me I can't drive my car? Can't own a gun? Can't have a second child, like in China?

I'm well acquainted with this type of response. Every year the Media Foundation tries to purchase airtime for its "Buy Nothing Day" TV campaign, which asks Americans to put away their wallets on the last Friday of November. Every year every major network turns our ad down, but one program—CNN *Headline News*—takes our money and runs our spot. Every year after the ad airs, dozens of irate viewers jam our 1-800 line. "Get out of this country, you pinko tree-huggers," one concerned citizen explained last year. "Go back to where you came from."

For an enormous number of people, the idea that they should set limits on themselves is unthinkable: "Why should I cut back? This is *my* paycheck, this is *my* life." Any restriction on this unfettered freedom to consume just does not square with the American dream. Our current economic system cannot tolerate any reduction in consumption. We simply cannot deal with that idea. *That is our rigidity.* And that is the kind of rigidity that brings civilizations down.

Meanwhile, back at the G-7 summit, the world leaders are putting on a good show for the thousands of journalists, reporters and TV crews. There are daily news releases, communiqués, background papers, joint declarations and photo ops. The PR people do their thing. A protest erupts as a few thousand people link hands and try to circle one of the leaders' meetings, but on TV this demonstration comes off as merely another part of the spectacle, somehow lending even more credibility to the event and reinforcing its importance and legitimacy.

The U.S. president reads some words prepared for him by his policy advisers. Millions around the world watch the proceedings on the evening news. We feel mildly reassured. These guys must know what they're doing. Despite the recent worrisome rumblings, the global economic vessel is on course. The unsinkable ship of dreams proceeds into the night. Inured, we grab the remote, switch away from the news and settle on *The X-Files*, where agent Fox Mulder is once again sniffing out some wild conspiracy.

spring

Paris, May 1968

THE REVOLUTIONARY IMPULSE

Most people in the world have never heard of culture jamming. Yet it is not a new movement. We place ourselves on a revolutionary continuum that includes, moving backward in time, early punk rockers, the '60s hippie movement, a group of European intellectuals and conceptual artists called the Situationist International (born of the Lettrist International), the surrealists, Dadaists, anarchists, and a host of other social agitators down through the ages whose chief aim was to challenge the prevailing ethos in a way that was so primal and heartfelt it could only be true.

What we all have in common—besides a belligerent attitude toward authority—is a willingness to take big risks, and a commitment to pursue small, spontaneous moments of truth. Opportunities to act boldly (which often means *not* the way you would normally, reflexively act) present themselves every day and maybe even every hour. Authentic acts tend to get noticed amid the fakery and correctness on which postmodern culture thrives. "In a small room where people unanimously maintain a conspiracy of silence," said Nobel laureate Czeslaw Milosz, "one word of truth sounds like a pistol shot."

In his book *Lipstick Traces*, American cultural critic Greil Marcus fixes The Sex Pistols' Johnny Rotten squarely in the tradition of the rebel seer. Rotten was a gleeful anarchist who used the word "fuck" on television and sang like he meant to change the world—or at least explode the dreamy, Beatles-fueled optimism of the day, and stick a fork into classic rock. He somehow rose above the obvious joke of The Pistols—the naked commercialism and hype of a band without much talent—and created something vital.

It's not clear whether Rotten knew anything about the Situationist International. But The Sex Pistols and the SI were most definitely on the same page, philosophically. Their song "Anarchy in the U.K." espoused, in crudely poetic form, the philosophy of the movement. The Pistols wanted to live "not as an object but as a subject of the story," as Marcus puts it. That's about as good a working definition of the culture jammers' ethos as you'll ever find.

Marcus recalls watching Johnny Rotten shouting madly over the band's guitars in front of the Berlin Wall and understanding that "his aim . . . was to take in all the rage, intelligence and strength in his being and then fling them back at the world; to make the world notice; to make the world doubt its most cherished and unexamined beliefs." I think culture jammers can learn a lot from the original punks. They were one of the first to feel the nihilism and to rail against a world that offered no future—and for a few years their rage shook the world.

The punks, like the hippies, yippies, beats, anarchists, Dadaists, surrealists, automatistes, fluxists and any number of other disaffected visionaries, represented an age-old spirit of spontaneous defiance toward the established order. But it was the Situationists who first applied that spirit of anarchy to modern media culture. They were the first to understand how the media spectacle slowly corrodes the human psyche. They were, in a sense, the first postmodern revolutionaries.

The Situationists were originally just eight artists and writers, most of them European, who sat down one July day in 1957 in the little town of Cosio d'Arroscia, Italy, to have a little fun together over Gauloises and absinthe. Though a reasonably short-lived group (by the '70s, most everyone had forgotten about them), they generated an anarchic drive that a generation of students, artists and radicals recognized as the real thing.

The Situationists declared a commitment to "a life of permanent novelty." They were interested only in freedom, and just about any means to it were justified. The creativity of everyday people, which consumer capitalism and communism had weakened but not killed, desperately needed to find expression. Down with the bureaucracies and hierarchies and ideologies that stifled spontaneity and free will. To the Situationists, you are—everyone is—a creator of situations, a performance artist, and the performance, of course, is your life, lived in your own way. Various stunts were concocted to foster spontaneous living. Situationist members suggested knocking down churches to make space for children to play, and putting switches on the street lamps so lighting would be under public control.

The Situationists believed that many times a day, each of us comes to a little fork in the path. We can then do one of two things: act the way we normally, reflexively act, or do something a little risky and wild, but genuine. We can choose to live our life as "a moral, poetic, erotic, and almost spiritual refusal" to cooperate with the demands of consumer culture.

The Situationists spoke often of the "spectacle" of modern life. The term encompassed everything from billboards to art exhibitions to soccer matches to radio and TV. Broadly speaking, it meant modern society's "spectacular" level of commodity consumption and hype. Everything human beings once experienced directly had been turned into a show put on by someone else. Real living had been replaced by prepackaged experiences and media-created events. Immediacy was gone. Now there was only "mediacy"—life as mediated through other instruments, life as a media creation. The Situationists used the term "kidnapped": The spectacle had "kidnapped" our real lives, co-opting whatever authenticity we once had.

I think this helps explain the strong visceral reaction so many people had to Nike's use of the Beatles tune "Revolution," and, later, to

Apple's appropriation of Bob Dylan and The Gap's (posthumous) mugging of Jack Kerouac. Nostalgic, griping yuppies may not have been able to articulate it perfectly, but they understood that some fundamental part of their lives had been stolen.

In the Richard Linklater film *Before Sunrise*, the young hero, played by Ethan Hawke, has an existential crisis: He suddenly grows sick to death of his own company. Every party he goes to, there he is. Every bus he rides, every class he attends, he runs into . . . himself. For him, even his own identity had somehow become a spectacle. Here Linklater is staring into the Situationist abyss, and finding it a little terrifying. To paraphrase Situationist leader Guy Debord: Where the self is by proxy, it is not. This may also explain why one of the juiciest consumer target groups is the man or woman known as the "emulator." Emulators look for products that make them feel like somebody else—someone more important. Since no product can help you fully escape your old identity, frustration mounts, a credit card is produced and the cycle of alienation deepens. (Situationists might point to emulators as proof of a devolution in the state of living: from "being" to "having," and then from "having" to "appearing to have.")

Debord remains a largely unheralded visionary. Derided in his later years, nearly canonized in France immediately following his suicide in 1967 and then gradually forgotten, Debord is only now enjoying a little posthumous fame—especially in France, where a group calling themselves the "Perpendiculaires" have positioned themselves as spiritual progeny of the Situationists. They maintain that culture ought to be spread laterally (through salon-type discussions) rather than vertically (through TV and the Internet).

In some ways, Debord was even more of a pioneer of the mental environment than his high-profile coeval, Marshall McLuhan. Where McLuhan only described the mass-culture trance, Debord developed some effective ways to break out of it. One way was the *dérive*. Literally "the drift," the *dérive* was an idea borrowed from the Dadaists. The Situationists defined it as "locomotion without a goal." As a *dériviste*, you float through the city, open to whatever you come in contact with, thus exposing yourself to the whole spectrum of feelings you encounter by chance in everyday life. Openness is key. You embrace whatever you love, and in the process, you discover what it is you hate.

The Situationists believed the *dérive* could largely replace the old twin occupations of work and entertainment, and become a model for the "playful creation" of a new way of life. The *dériviste* is a drifter in the best possible sense, not someone down and out but up and beyond, living outside the stifling roles society prescribes for us. Living well, Debord said, involves the "systematic questioning of all the diversions and works of a society, a total critique of its idea of happiness."

Another of the Situationists' favorite tropes was *détournement*, which Debord proposed as a way for people to take back the spectacle that had kidnapped their lives. Literally a "turning around," *détournement* involved rerouting spectacular images, environments, ambiences and events to reverse or subvert their meaning, thus reclaiming them. With its limitless supply of ideas, ranging from rewriting the speech balloons of comic-strip characters, to altering the width of streets and the heights of buildings and the colors and shapes of doors and windows, to radically reinterpreting world events such as the 1965 Watts riots in Los Angeles, the *Internationale Situationniste*—the journal the Situationists published between 1958 and 1969—was a sometimes profound, sometimes absurd laboratory of provocation and *détournement*. Once, Debord altered a famous drawing of Lenin by placing a barebreasted woman on his forehead with the caption "The Universe Turns on the Tips of Breasts." Debord had his book *Mémoires* bound in heavy sandpaper so that when it was placed on the shelves of libraries, it would destroy other books. One famous *détournement* happened in the Notre Dame cathedral on Easter Sunday in 1950. With thousands of people watching, a Lettrist provocateur dressed as a Dominican monk slipped onto the altar and delivered a sermon accusing the Catholic Church of "the deadly diversion of the force of life in favor of an empty heaven," and then solemnly proclaimed that "God is dead." It was with this spirit of *détournement* that the Situationists invaded enemy territory and tried to "devalue the currency of the spectacle." And it was with this defiance that they intended to pull off a cultural revolution, "a gigantic turning around of the existing social world."

The Situationists had some fairly radical notions that, when you consider them deeply, make sense. They believed that vacations, so cherished by the masses as a kind of sanity-saver, instead just enforce "the loop of alienation and domination" and symbolize "the false promises of modern life." (If you're living a full life, why would you want to "get away" from it?) A memorable neo-Situationist slogan reads: "Club Med, a Cheap Holiday in Other People's Misery."

In *The Revolution of Everyday Life,* which apart from Debord's *The Society of Spectacle* is the seminal book to emerge from the Situationist movement, Raul Vaneigem argued that everyday life is ultimately the measure of all things, and the ground on which all revolutions must unfold. But, he argued, an unfortunate, alienating self-consciousness has crept into our lives. "Even the tiniest of gestures—opening a door, holding a teacup, a facial expression—and the most private and individual actions—coming home, making tea, arguing with a lover—have always already been represented and shown to us within the spectacle." Thus, our most intimate gestures have become stereotypes, and our lives clichéd. But Vaneigem passionately believed that the spectacle was fast approaching a saturation point, a crisis out of which "a new poetry of real experience and a reinvention of life are bound to spring."

Today, the stultifying passivity and alienation of the spectacle in our lives has increased to proportions Vaneigem and Debord could hardly have imagined. The great, insidious power of the spectacle lies in the fact that it is actually a form of mental slavery that we are free to resist, *only it never occurs to us to do so.* Our media-saturated postmodern world, where all communication flows in one direction, from the powerful to the powerless, produces a population of lumpen spectators "modern men and women, the citizens of the most advanced societies on earth, thrilled to watch whatever it is they're given to watch."

Greil Marcus calls this the "democracy of false desire." The spectacle is an instrument of social control, offering the illusion of unlimited choice, but in fact reducing the field of play to a choice of preselected experiences: adventure movies, nature shows, celebrity romances, political scandals, ball games, net surfing. . . .

Boredom emerges in the Situationist literature as one of the Big Enemies. The Situationists saw a world crushed by wasted potential. Mass mechanization, for example, was supposed to create vast stretches of leisure time in which people could create free-flowing, imaginative lives for themselves. Instead, people were allowing their leisure hours to be gobbled up by programmed entertainments. Increasingly, they weren't in control of their own fun anymore. The Situationist solution: *Take back the show.* Create your own atmospheres, ambiences and situations. Build something "provisional and lived." One might, to cite one example, take the predictable city and redesign it as a bunch of emotive neighborhoods—the "bizarre" quarter, the "sinister" quarter, the "tragic" quarter, the "happy" quarter, and the "useful" quarter—that people can drift in and out of.

Whatever else you might think of Guy Debord—that he was wildly idealistic and extreme in his views—he did walk the walk. He created a life free of spectacle (except right at the end when, sick and in pain, he carefully orchestrated his own spectacular suicide by a gunshot through the heart). He never had a job; he spent his time in taverns, arguing philosophy, drinking and writing. He consistently refused interviews with the press and wrote only six slim volumes. "I wrote much less than most people who write, but drank much more than most people who drink," he once remarked. For him life really *was* an eternal festival. He believed passionately in his own destiny and that of his friends. "Our kind will be the first to blaze a trail into a new life," he boasted.

The heroes of the Situationists' era were unbridled and anarchical, pure vessels of poetic expression, living somehow out of time. They were the polar opposite of the people often held up as examples in our own age of workaholism—competitive, ambitious folks who, as Welsh historian L.T.C. Rolt put it in his classic book *High Horse Riderless*, "believe in faster trains and more traffic, who ravage the landscape while claiming to protect it, who disintegrate the family while assuring us it is their priority, who sanctify work while increasing unemployment. All this because they have jettisoned faith in the true spiritual nature of the human being and have not the courage to risk being real, but must always be striving to become superior to their competitors."

The cognitive psychologist Abraham Maslow spoke of the importance of peak experiences in the life of a fully functioning, or "self-actualized," human being. These experiences are so engrossing to the senses—in this instant, this act—that people actually feel they are living out of time. Other disciplines have other names for it. Zen Buddhists call peak experiences *satori*. "Generations of poets, prophets, and revolutionaries, not to mention lovers, drug-takers, and all those who have somehow found the time to stand and stare" have craved this ecstatic feeling of oneness with the world. This is also why many culture jammers take daily leaps of faith, or of courage—acts that take them outside market-structured consciousness long enough to get a taste of real living. Living in the moment, pursuing the authentic gesture, living close to the edge—call it what you will—when it's genuine, it's the force that makes life worth living. It is also what consumer capitalism takes away from you every time it sells you brand-name "cool" or this month's rebel attitude.

When I was shooting a film in Japan called *Satori in the Right Cortex,* I asked the head monk of a Zen monastery in Kamakura if I could take footage of his disciples meditating. Yes, he said, but first *you* must meditate. He wasn't talking about a quick *namaste* and a couple of mumbled koans. He meant sitting for two full days. So I took him up on his challenge. I sat on the floor meditating until my back stiffened, joints ached and muscles cramped. It was physical and psychological torture—a hell I will never forget. But by the end of the second day something really had changed. The monk had forced a painful interruption in my soft routine, and I emerged humbled, thankful and, for a few hours, euphoric. Maybe only when you're shoved into a new pattern of behavior and make the commitment not to back out—when your hand is held to the fire or you hold your own hand to the fire—do the real gains come. When the trance is interrupted, you catch a brief, tantalizing glimpse of the way life could be.

What does this have to do with revolution and culture jamming? Everything. Interrupting the stupefyingly comfortable patterns we've fallen into isn't pleasant or easy. It's like crawling out of your warm bed in your dark room one December morning at five A.M. and plunging into a tub of ice water. It shocks the system. But sometimes shock is what a system needs. It's certainly what our bloated, self-absorbed consumer culture needs.

Culture jamming is, at root, just a metaphor for stopping the flow of spectacle long enough to adjust your set. Stopping the flow relies on an element of surprise. That's why a Zen master may suddenly throw you a wildly cryptic, inappropriate, even obscene answer to your harmless query. He might answer your question by removing his shoe and placing it on top of his head, or throwing it at you, or telling you that if you meet Buddha on the road you must kill him. The Zen master is trying to break your trance. He's showing you a new path to the waterfall. Debord called this kind of thing "breaking the old syntax," and replacing it with a new one. The new syntax carries the instructions for "a whole new way of being in the world."

What does the perceptual shift feel like when it comes? Imagine a desperately down-and-out soul who suddenly finds God. Now try to imagine the *opposite* of that process. This moment of reckoning is not so much like suddenly seeing heaven in a world you thought was hell as it is suddenly seeing hell in a world you thought was heaven. That world is the world of summer blockbusters and $5 lattes and Super Bowls in which a thirty-second ad slot sells for $1.5 million—the spectacular world of the American dream, a world you were raised to believe was the best of all worlds, but a world that collapses under scrutiny. If you stare at your reflection in the mirror long enough, your face becomes a monster's face, with enormous sunken gargoyle eyes.

In the 1998 film *The Truman Show*, a corporation adopts Truman Burbank at birth, then carefully scripts a whirl of product placement and impression management into his life, which is televised live, twenty-four hours a day. The only time Truman upsets that managed order, when he catches a glimpse of the real world behind his scripted life, is when he does something spontaneous. Slowly, he comes to realize that only a chain of spontaneous acts will lead to salvation. The culture jammer is seized by a similar sense of urgency to do something, anything, to escape the consumerist script.

Buddhist mythology tells the tale of Buddha's enlightenment. In the beginning Buddha is a plump, rich fellow living in an opulent palace. Occasionally, on his walks around the grounds, he spies, through fissures in the palace walls, the world of suffering, pain and disease. He is repulsed, but also mesmerized. Eventually, he decides to leave the palace and live in that real world. There's a lesson here for jammers about how to snap the First World out of its media-consumer trance. Each time the flow of images and information is interrupted—by any spontaneous, individual act, or any act of mass-media *détournement*— it's like the Buddha catching a glimpse through the palace wall. Over time—say five or ten years—the glimpses add up to a fairly detailed picture of life outside the palace.

If enough people saw the light and undertook spontaneous acts at once, the Situationists believed, the result would be a mass awakening that would suddenly devalue the currency of the spectacle. "The détournement of the right sign, in the right place at the right time, could spark a mass reversal of perspective," Greil Marcus said. Suddenly, the spectacle would be exposed in all its emptiness. Everyone would see through it.

This is how the spell is broken. This is how the revolution begins: A few people start slipping out of old patterns, daydreaming, questioning, rebelling. What happens naturally then, the Situationists believed, is a groundswell of support for this new way of being, with more and more people empowered to perform new gestures "unencumbered by history." The new generation, the Situationists believed, "would leave nothing to chance."

Those words still haunt us. The society of spectacle has triumphed. The American dream has devolved into exactly the vacant obliviousness they talked about—a have-a-nice-day kind of happiness that close examination tends to disturb. If you keep up appearances, keep yourself diverted with new acquisitions and constant entertainments, keep your-self pharmacologized and recoil the moment you feel real life seeping in between the cracks, you'll be all right.

Some dream.

If the old American dream was about prosperity, maybe the new one will be about spontaneity.

The Situationists maintained that ordinary people have all the tools they need for revolution. The only thing missing is a perceptual shift—a tantalizing glimpse of a new way of being—that suddenly brings everything into focus.

THE NEW ACTIVISM (FIRE IN THE BELLY)

You may already be a culture jammer. Maybe you're a student who does not want a career working for corporate America. A graphic artist tired of selling your soul to ad agency clients. A vegan. A biker. A maverick professor. An Earth Firster who liberated a billboard last night.

We jammers are a loose global network of artists, activists, environmentalists, Green entrepreneurs, media-literacy teachers, downshifters, reborn Lefties, high-school shit disturbers, campus rabble-rousers, dropouts, incorrigibles, poets, philosophers, ecofeminists. We cover the spectrum from the cool intellectual middle to the violent lunatic fringe, from Raging Grannies who chant doggerel at protests to urban guerrillas who stage wild street parties. We are ecological economists, TV jammers, ethical investors. We paint our own bike lanes, reclaim streets, "skull" Calvin Klein ads, and paste GREASE stickers on tables and trays at McDonald's restaurants. We organize swap meets, rearrange items on supermarket shelves, make our software available free on the Net, and generally apply ourselves to the daily business of getting consumer culture to bite its own tail. We're idealists, anarchists, guerrilla tacticians, hoaxers, pranksters, neo-Luddites, malcontents and punks. We are the

ragtag remnants of oppositional culture—what's left of the revolutionary impulse in the jaded "*fin de millénium* atmosphere of postmodernity" in which revolution is said to be no longer possible. What we share
is an overwhelming rage against consumer capitalism, and a vague
sense that our time has come to act as a collective force.

On the simplest level, we are a growing band of people who have
given up on the American dream. Here are a few samples of the way we
think:

- Instead of treating vegetative, corporate-driven TV culture as
  something to be gently, ironically mocked, it's time to face the
  whole ugly specter of our TV-addicted nation, the savage anomie
  of a society entranced and entrapped and living a lie. It's time to
  admit that chronic TV watching is North America's number one
  mental health problem, and that a society in which citizens spend a
  quarter of their waking lives (more than four hours a day) in front
  of their sets is in serious need of shock therapy.

- We recycle our beer cans, newspapers and vodka bottles; we join
  car pools and food co-ops; we turn our thermostats down at night.
  We do all the right things. So why do our environmental problems
  just keep getting worse? Maybe it's time we stopped expending our
  energies on small do-goody gestures and faced the fact that many
  of the paradigms within which we live—cultural, social, economic—are outdated and dysfunctional. Most of our environmental "solutions" are red herrings. They deflect energy from the
  essential work at hand. What we need is not just fewer cars on the
  roads but new cities designed chiefly with pedestrians, bicycles and
  public transport in mind. Not just new ecofriendly products, but
  new consumption patterns and new lifestyles. Not just a carbon
  tax, but a global across-the-board pricing system that tells the ecological truth. Not just new measures of economic progress more
  accurate than the GDP, but a radical rethinking of the neoclassical
  paradigm we've been teaching in Economics 101 for the past few
  generations.

- Ours is a society filled with exceptional individuals, affluent communities, efficient businesses, top-notch universities and exciting cities. But that is no longer enough. The concept of excellence must now be applied to the *whole* culture. We have never been afraid of getting tough with the other broken systems in our lives; we retrain workers, dump governments, and eagerly, completely revamp entire corporate cultures such as IBM's when they lose their sense of mission. Now let's apply that same sense of focused urgency to the repair of our culture.

    Let's rethink our vital components—our information delivery systems, our basic ideas about nutrition, transportation and economics. Let's commit, totally, passionately, to reducing our ecological footprint, to learning how to measure progress accurately, to countering the information viruses spreading in our midst. Instead of resisting this kind of fundamental change, let's embrace it. Let's cheer on our cultural rebels even as we fear them. Let's revel in (or at least not shy away from) the life and death of our paradigms.

But more exactly, more precisely, what do we culture jammers actually *stand* for? What do we want? Perhaps the best way to explain and define ourselves is to be clear about who—or what—we *aren't*.

We're Not Cool

"Cool" used to mean unique, spontaneous, compelling. The coolest kid was the one everyone wanted to be like but no one quite could, because her individuality was utterly distinct. Then "cool" changed. Marketers got hold of it and reversed its meaning. Now you're cool if you are *not* unique—if you have the look and feel that bear the unmistakable stamp of America™. Hair by Paul Mitchell. Khakis by The Gap. Car by BMW. Attitude by Nike. Pet phrases by Letterman. Politics by Bill Maher. Cool is the opiate of our time, and over a couple of generations, we have grown dependent on it to maintain our identities of inclusion.

Legitimately cool people instinctively understand that the psychology of subservience—getting corporately seduced—is a chicken-ass way to live. Today, such people are an endangered species.

What's cool now? Same as always: It's cool to rebel. But a lot of people who think they're rebelling, aren't. It's quite a trick the Culture Trust has pulled off, to offer, as *The Baffler* editor Tom Frank puts it, "Establishment and Resistance in one convenient package." We think we're buying anarchy when what we're actually buying is just corporate-crafted conformity. We're buying a rebel template instead of creating our own.

Let's face it: When you dress to the nines, drive to the max and order a bottle of Cabernet Sauvignon that costs more than a weekend in New England, you're just showing off. And, as Harvard economist Juliet Schor pointed out in *The Overspent American*, showing off in this way is, ultimately, a political act.

An increasing number of people are growing uncomfortable with the gulf between the world's rich and poor. Ostentatiously splashing your money around simply draws attention to that disparity, and to your own position on the lucky high ground. It suggests a callousness, an inhumanity, a let's-just-rub-their-noses-in-it arrogance.

Inegalitarianism and exclusiveness are not cool. First World opulence is not cool. A culture that keeps hyping people to consume more is not cool. America™ is not cool. And the people who fall for the hype are the worst kind of uncool: They're suckers.

We're Not Slackers

The generation of North Americans born between 1965 and 1980—in Canadian writer Hal Niedzviecki's coinage, the "Malaise Generation"—seems to have pretty much given up hope that any good will come of this place called Earth. Taken as a group (and there are of course some exceptional overachievers within this group—exceptions that prove the rule), this generation represents the biggest waste of potential energy, passion, creativity and intellect in our time. This generation, which in primitive societies would have done the bulk of the tribe's work, has voluntarily removed itself from the collective effort because . . . hey, what's the point? Slackers spend days on end sharpening their sardonic edge on the whetstone of apathy. They philosophize on the meaning of a Kraft Dinner, they fish Hush Puppies from the discount bins of Wal-Mart or, in a burst of inspiration, they issue zines with names like *A.d.i.d.a.s* (*All Day I Dream About Suicide*). To slackers, the worst crime is to admit to being committed to anything, because then you appear earnest, and earnest ain't ironic. It ain't cool. So maybe it's better just to drift down to Santa Monica, to "sit beside the ocean and watch the world die."

Meanwhile, on the American campus—the great waiting room, the traditional place for radical demonstrations to rage—not much is happening. While Indonesian, Chinese, and Korean students fight corruption and injustice and shake up their nations, North American undergrads doze in the library. There's no real rush to finish a degree because what lies on the other side but debt, pavement pounding and the potential shame of boomeranging back home?

Members of the Malaise Generation understand that they—we—are all dupes of the consumer culture. They understand. They just aren't willing to do anything about it. And that's where I lose patience with them; that's when an irrepressible anger wells up. "Life sucks." Okay. So fix a small corner of it. When so much is at stake, how can you be so complacent?

We're Not Academic

Why do we feel so confused and uncertain? Where do our malaise and cynicism come from? What's wrong with the affluent West? There's been no shortage of analysis. In academic journals and on TV panel shows, scientists and pundits offer their theories and explanations. They've studied the psychological and physical dimensions of the problem and laid the cards on the table. Mood disorders are rising and male sperm counts are falling, due to chemical pollution of our air, water and food. But the scientists warn us not to confuse correlation with causation, not to jump to conclusions. A full understanding of these recent phenomena requires further research, more testing, more funds. The global temperature is rising because our cars are pumping too much carbon into the atmosphere. But we cannot allow ourselves to get too alarmed just yet. We need to study this further before we can be sure. There are links between exposure to diesel fumes and asthma, between chronic TV viewing and the desire to snooze all day. This merits serious investigation. Many areas of our society can be shown to be deficient in all manner of ways and here, ladies and gentlemen, are the graphs.

Moat academics just ramble. Far too few raise a fist or a voice. Communications professors tell their students everything that's wrong with the global media monopoly, but never a word about how to fix it. Economics professors drone on endlessly about their macroeconomic models while in the real world we live off the planet's natural capital and the backs of future generations.

We in the affluent West—the children of Socrates, Plato, Pascal, Descartes, Hegel, Nietzsche, Marx and Wittgenstein—now live almost exclusively in the left cortex of our brains. The dominant personality in our culture is the logic freak: the macroeconomist, the biotechnician, the investment guru, the computer whiz; the dispassionate thinker. Mesmerized by binary options—black and white, good and bad, right and wrong, heaven and hell, 1 and 0—we've become a *McLaughlin Group* culture. We just talk. We don't actually do anything. And why should we? Why would the people living the cushiest lives on the planet want anything to change? Why should we spoil our sinecure when we can pretend to be deeply concerned, keep the analysis humming and the big salaries and consulting fees rolling in?

Thousands of delegates descend on Rio, Kyoto and New York City for the Earth summits, generating tons of garbage and exhaust. Strong statements are made, reams of reports are generated. The delegates enjoy multicourse dinners of regional cuisine. Nothing changes.

Nonexperts—regular reasonable people—are disgusted by all this dithering. They already have a pretty good idea of what's going on. They can tell by the issues their politicians choose *not* to address. By the hurricanes and floods that signal a rearrangement of the heavy furniture of the ecosystem. By the surge of robotic consumption in the malls at Christmastime. By the way their kids' expressions grow vacant by the third hour of television viewing.

Abbie Hoffman nailed it when, after being told that academics and experts were busy analyzing the subject of "subversive activity," he said: "What the fuck you analyzin' for, man? Get in and do it!" And Edward Abbey nailed it when he said: "Sentiment without action is the ruin of the soul."

We're Not Feminists

I remember well how passionate, exciting and outrageous feminists were in the '60s and '70s, how they challenged just about every aspect of the way we lived. Most clearly, I remember the hope and direction they gave me and my generation.

But, perhaps a casualty of its own considerable success, feminism has now become an ideology, a strangely irrelevant "ism" stuck in another era, too narrowly focused on its own special interests and increasingly divided against itself. I knew feminism was in trouble about ten years ago when I saw a WOMEN ONLY sign hanging over a drop-in center doorway at Vancouver's Simon Fraser University. Relentless attention to small, self-serving issues has deflected attention from the broader questions of what's fundamentally wrong with our culture as a whole. For too many of the feminists I meet today, at conferences, brainstorming sessions and in my work as editor of *Adbusters,* everything automatically boils down to a gender issue. I just can't buy that.

Feminism still holds great intellectual power, and I am sure it will continue to play a crucial role in softening up the male fiefdoms of science, medicine and philosophy, and in promoting holism and a more intimate relationship with the natural world. Recently, the insightful audacity of a few eco- and cyberfeminists—Suzi Gablik, Donna Haraway and Sadie Plant among them—has surprised and delighted me and reminded me of the old glory days. Perhaps they, and others like them, will rise above the current self-absorption of feminist politics and unleash a new wave of cultural excitement over the world. But, by and large, feminism today has ceased being a broad-based social movement and become just one of many special interest "victim" groups vying for a piece of the money and the action.

We're Not Lefties

Many jammers, including myself, were raised on, embraced and felt most comfortable with the ideas of the Left. But for about fifteen years now, the Left has been letting us down. It has become tired, self-satisfied and dogmatic. (I think of Allen Ginsberg, who found that his mother's simplistic Left-wing views left him suspicious of both sides.) Back in the '50s and '60s, the Left was visionary and fearless. Today the fire in its belly has gone out. It isn't getting the job done.

What happened?

Certainly, the collapse of the Soviet empire undermined the Left's whole philosophical base. Government control, central planning, public ownership (and by extension the welfare state and social democracy) were all shown to be fundamentally flawed. Today, nations are purging these ideological remnants and adopting free-market philosophies. Those philosophies are also seriously flawed, but they are far better than centralized government control of every aspect of economic life. When I saw the wholesale ecological devastation that the Communist era had left behind, I stopped calling myself a Lefty right then and there.

But old Lefties die hard.

We find in *Mother Jones, The Nation, Z, Extra, The Multinational Monitor* and dozens of Left-sprung books, magazines and newsletters the same old authors repeating the same old ideas of yesteryear. It isn't that many of these writers aren't fine journalists, or don't have a solid grasp of the issues, it's just that they lack passion. There's something drab and predictable about them; they feel like losers. (This reminds me of my Japanese friends in Tokyo at the peak of their economic miracle circa 1970, scratching their heads in amazement when I showed them a picture of Jesus Christ on the cross. "This cannot be a god," they said. "He looks too much like a loser to be a god.")

Each year Sonoma State University issues its list of the ten most censored stories of the year (the endeavor has spun off to Canada as well), but "Project Censored" is shouting into a void, and the list of censored stories it picks every year reads like yet another ideological wish list. The Public Interest Research Group (PIRG) system set up in universities by Ralph Nader's Raiders twenty-five years ago is still chugging along on the tired steam of its old agendas, but its bravest battles are behind it. Many of the Left's great inspirational voices— Lasch, Berger, Heilbroner, Galbraith—have died or are *in extremis*. The vacuum has been filled by tenured professors, TV pundits and self-proclaimed champions of oppositional culture. I've had dealings with many of these people: They no longer pine for real change. For them fundamental change is just a utopian dream, and if it suddenly happened they wouldn't know what to do with it. They're content to give another speech at another symposium, or write yet another humorless article ridiculing the far Right. Left activists, even some of the best, have been reduced to the level of little kids throwing snowballs at passing cars.

Harper's editor Lewis Lapham is the quintessential liberal Lefty. Every month he passionately and often eloquently dissects the moral state of the union. But when *Adbusters* challenged him on the ethics of running tobacco advertisements in his own magazine, he steadfastly refused to be drawn into the debate. For years he stonewalled our letters, phone calls and entreaties, and played a cat-and-mouse game with us in the media. He couldn't face up to a moral indignity in his own yard.

The liberal Left has a way of co-opting every worthwhile cause. In the past few decades, it has hung its flag on the black movement, the women's movement and the environmental movement. It has muscled in on every major struggle and social protest of the past half century. But no longer are Lefties fighting the problem, they *are* the problem,

and if we're going to build an effective new social movement, we're going to have to work not with them but around them.

The critical issues of our time are neither Left nor Right, neither male nor female, neither black nor white. The challenge for new millennium activists is to find the courage to let go of all their old orthodoxies, "isms" and sacred cows, and to commit to "a ruthless criticism of all that exists." And after that, the big challenge is to bring revolutionary consciousness and contestation back into the modern world by standing up and boldly announcing to the world what Parisian rebels declared some thirty years ago: "We will wreck this world."

THE MEME WARS

A meme (rhymes with "dream") is a unit of information (a catchphrase, a concept, a tune, a notion of fashion, philosophy or politics) that leaps from brain to brain to brain. Memes compete with one another for replication, and are passed down through a population much the same way genes pass through a species. Potent memes can change minds, alter behavior, catalyze collective mindshifts and transform cultures. Which is why meme warfare has become the geopolitical battle of our information age. Whoever has the memes has the power.

Activists can stage sit-ins, organize massive protests and stage mighty battles with riot police. But these events will at best flicker briefly on the evening news and be gone with no demonstrable change in the world. They are spectacles with radium half-lives. The real riots, the important ones that shift alliances, shake governments, win (or lose) elections and force corporations and industries to rethink their agendas, now take place inside your head.

The next revolution—World War III—will be, as Marshall McLuhan predicted, "a guerrilla information war" fought not in the sky or on the streets, not in the forests or around international fishing boundaries on the high seas, but in newspapers and magazines, on the radio, on TV and in cyberspace. It will be a dirty, no-holds-barred propaganda war of competing worldviews and alternative visions of the future.

We jammers can win this battle for ourselves and for Planet Earth. Here's how:

We build our own meme factory, put out a better product and beat the corporations at their own game. We identify the macromemes and the metamemes—the core ideas without which a sustainable future is unthinkable—and deploy them.

Here are five of the most potent metamemes currently in the culture jammer's arsenal:

True Cost: In the global marketplace of the future, the price of every product will tell the ecological truth.

Demarketing: The marketing enterprise has now come full circle. The time has come to *unsell* the product and turn the incredible power of marketing against itself.

The Doomsday Meme: The global economy is a doomsday machine that must be stopped and reprogrammed.

No Corporate "I": Corporations are not legal "persons" with constitutional rights and freedoms of their own, but legal fictions that we ourselves created and must therefore control.

Media Carta: Every human being has the "right to communicate"—to receive and impart information through any media.

What would happen if even 10 percent of North Americans came to believe in and support even one of these ideas? Life would change. The ready-for-prime-time metameme—the big paradigm-busting idea that suddenly captures the public imagination and becomes a super-spectacle in itself—is the meme-warfare equivalent of a nuclear bomb. It causes cognitive dissonance of the highest order. It jolts people out of their habitual patterns and nudges society in brave new directions.

The last time social activists ventured wholesale into TV, they won a magnificent victory. I'm talking about the tobacco war, which history will record as having begun in the 1960s and having ended around the turn of the millennium, with the tobacco giants finally rolling over. The tobacco war marked the first (and so far the last) time anti-ads beat product ads in open meme combat in a free marketplace of ideas.

Here was a multibillion-dollar industry butting heads with the fledgling antitobacco lobby. In 1969, the antitobacco crusaders, through persistent efforts and relentless pressure, managed to secure airtime for their antismoking ads, which ran against the cigarette ads that were then still legal on TV.

I remember those ads vividly—the superclose-ups of the glowing tips of cigarettes, the X rays of cruddy lungs. I remember Yul Brynner, whose last creative act in the world, after a slow disintegration from lung cancer, was to come on TV just months from death, look the world squarely in the eye and say, "Whatever you do, don't smoke." That meme forged the link between cigarettes and death. Everybody watching knew it was the truth. Those anti-ads helped me and millions of others to quit smoking. More significantly, they demonstrated that even a multibillion-dollar cartel can be beaten in a free marketplace of ideas.

The antismoking meme crushed the smoking meme. Even with all its financial might, the tobacco industry was simply unable to compete because it lost its psychological stranglehold on the public mind. It lost its magic. Smoking was uncooled, and no amount of PR money could buy the cool back. In 1971, the tobacco companies "voluntarily" accepted a federal ban on TV and radio cigarette advertising, and their ads have not appeared in those media since.

For the antismoking lobby—early culture jammers—beating the enemy on TV was the key. The victory initiated the great social turn-around of the next twenty years, with smokers in increasing numbers being driven out of the temple.

Today a new generation of jammers is inspired by that victory. If the mighty tobacco industry was vulnerable to calculated, well-researched,

AUTOSAURUS
30-SECOND TV SPOT

A woman's hand sensually caresses a shiny new car.

Suddenly, the car morphs into an Autosaurus, a terrifying robotic dinosaur, made of hulks of old cars.

Voice: "It's coming, it's coming . . . the most significant event in automotive history . . . the end of the age of the automobile."

The Autosaurus screeches and collapses into a heap.

Voice:
"Imagine a world with less cars."

tactical assaults by TV activists, then surely such subversive efforts can be repeated with success on other dysfunctional industries.

Jammers are now mobilizing to repeat the tobacco story in many other areas of life. We're going to take on the global automakers, the chemical companies, the food industries, the fashion corporations and the pop-culture marketeers in a free-information environment. We believe we can launch a new brand and beat America™ in a meme war. We're better organized and much smarter than we were twenty-five years ago. I like our odds.

Culture Jammer's Manifesto

We will take on the
archetypal mind polluters
and beat them at their
own game.

We will uncool their
billion-dollar brands
with uncommercials
on TV, subvertisements
in magazines and anti-ads
right next to theirs in
the urban landscape.

We will seize control of
the roles and functions
that corporations play
in our lives and set new
agendas in their industries.

We will jam the pop-culture
marketeers and bring their
image factory to a sudden,
shuddering halt.

On the rubble of the old
culture, we will build a new
one with a non-commercial
heart and soul.

THE MEME WARRIOR

Next time you're in a particularly soul-searching mood, ask yourself this simple question: What would it take for me to make a spontaneous, radical gesture in support of something I believe in? Do I believe in *anything* strongly enough? What would it take for me to say, This may not be nice, it may not be considerate, it may not even be rational—but damn it, I'm going to do it anyway because it feels right? I'm going to take this pair of scissors and cut my credit card in half. I'm going to take this little doll I've bought out of its huge box, right here at Toys "R" Us, and leave the wasteful packaging on the counter. Next time I'm caught standing in a long line at the bank, I'm going to shout cheerfully: "Hey, how about opening another teller!"

Direct action is a proclamation of personal independence. It happens, for the first time, at the intersection of your self-consciousness and your tolerance for being screwed over. You act. You thrust yourself forward and intervene. And then you hang loose and deal with whatever comes. In that moment of decision, in that leap into the unknown, you come to life. Your interior world is suddenly vivid. You're like a cat on the prowl: alive, alert and still a little wild.

It's fun to wrestle with titans. It's exhilarating to throw a megacorporation like McDonald's or Nike or Calvin Klein to the mat with the awesome momentum of its own icons and marketing hype—leveraging the very brand recognition the company so painstakingly built over the years. It's a fascinating exercise to take on a cartel like the global automakers and try to make it question its mandate. It's empowering to try to force a whole academic discipline like neoclassical economics to rethink its axioms.

In any such fight the underdog is perfectly positioned to take risks and test theories. Culture jammers are continually trying out new strategic ploys in the meme wars. Here are a few we've found so far.

Leverage Points

Almost every social problem, no matter how seemingly intractable, can be solved with enough time, scrutiny and effort. There's always some little fissure you can squeeze a crowbar into and heave. That's the leverage point. When pressure is applied there, memes start replicating, minds start changing and, in time, the whole culture moves.

There's a story often told by systems analysts—including Donella Meadows, coauthor of *Limits to Growth*—to illustrate how a little action at a system's leverage point can make all the difference in the world. The manager of a housing co-op was growing increasingly frustrated with her tenants. No matter how much she reminded and badgered them, no matter how many meetings she convened, no matter how much good-will there was for the task, the tenants would not, could not reduce their energy consumption. Finally she hit on an idea. What would happen, she wondered, if the electricity meters were moved from the basement to a conspicuous spot right beside the front door, so that each time the tenants left or entered their home they could see how fast their meter was whirring?

The meters were moved. Lo and behold, within a few weeks electricity consumption fell 30 percent.

This tale inspires culture jammers because it reminds us of what our movement is all about: *finding that leverage point.* Something is wrong; it can be fixed, but the fix requires seeing the situation in a novel way. "It's not a parameter adjustment, not a strengthening or weakening of an existing loop," says Meadows. "It's a *new loop* delivering feedback to a place where it wasn't going before."

How do you get society to make do with fewer cars? You can encourage people to make bicycles a bigger part of their lives. You can organize "Bike to Work" weeks. You can pay employers to subsidize commuters who pedal in from the suburbs. All of these things will certainly help. But the leverage point may turn out to be an idea that uncools one of the core rituals of car culture—the Indy 500. We uncooled beauty pageants, why not Indy races? Both are relics of a bygone era.

Other examples abound. When citizens are in the grip of fashion chic, you can "skull" fashion billboards, you can organize national "Fashin' Bashin' Weeks," you can point people toward thrift stores. But if you concentrate your energies on one fashion mogul—I suggest Calvin Klein—and try to uncool his line and logo, then you may have found a way to leverage the whole industry. An activist-induced drop in cK sales of even a few percent would signal that the tables have turned.

Leverage points are easier to find if you brainstorm and are ready to act on a grand scale. Why not go head to head with the junk-food industry on TV? Why not take legal action against TV broadcasters who won't sell you airtime? Why not take your case to the World Court? Why not try to launch a global media reform movement? Why not try to revoke Philip Morris's corporate charter?

Détournement

Corporations advertise. Culture jammers *sub*vertise. A well-produced print "subvertisement" mimics the look and feel of the target ad, prompting the classic double take as viewers realize what they're seeing is in fact the very opposite of what they expected. Subvertising is potent mustard. It cuts through the hype and glitz of our mediated reality and momentarily, tantalizingly, reveals the hollow spectacle within.

Suppose you don't have the money to launch a real print ad campaign. What you *can* do is mimic the million-dollar look and feel of your opponent's campaign, thereby *détourning* their own carefully worked out, button-pushing memes in your favor. They spend millions building their corporate cool, and you keep stealing their electricity.

Cyberjamming

The Internet is one of the most potent meme-replicating mediums ever invented. With cyberspace growing at about the rate of an infant—doubling in size every ten months—and with users always looking to pass on a scoop, good memes reproduce furiously. In 1997, Buy Nothing Day grew from a relatively small counterculture event in the Pacific Northwest to one of the biggest outbursts of anticonsumer sentiment the world has ever seen. Anyone with a PC and a modem could go to the Media Foundation's website (www.adbusters.org), download a Buy Nothing Day poster and a T-shirt template, and view quicktime versions of the Buy Nothing Day TV campaign. And hundreds of thousands did.

Cyberjamming is evolving at a dizzying pace. Here are a few interesting techniques in use at the time of this writing:

Cyberpetitions
Don't wear out your shoes trying to collect hard-copy signatures in person. Instead, use the Internet to gain immediate access to millions of like-minded souls to consider your proposal, sign your petition and e-mail it back to you.

Virtual Protests
Link people who visit your website directly to the site of your quarry (be it Monsanto, McDonald's, Philip Morris or NBC), where they can find creative ways to lodge a protest.

Virtual Sit-ins

Immobilize an enemy site by organizing a few dozen cyberjammers simultaneously to request more texts, pictures, animations and multimedia elements than the site can handle.

Gripe Sites

Create and maintain a site dedicated to uncooling one particular corporation or brand.

TV Jamming

A fifteen-, thirty- or sixty-second TV spot created by a team of passionate filmmakers is, I believe, the most powerful of all the weapons in the culture jammer's arsenal. I sometimes call a well-conceived and -produced social marketing TV message a "mindbomb" because of how it explodes in the collective psyche, sending out shock waves of cognitive dissonance. An effective TV subvertisement (or uncommercial) is so unlike what surrounds it on the commercial-TV mindscape that it immediately grabs the attention of viewers. It breaks their media-consumer trance and momentarily challenges their whole world outlook. It's guerrilla meme warfare on the most powerful social communications medium of our time. It can catch whole industries by surprise, trigger government policy reviews, derail legislation, launch new political initiatives. A thirty-second TV campaign is a legitimate way for a private citizen or activist group to challenge government, corporate and industrial agendas. And the idea that *you* have the right to do that in a democracy is utterly empowering.

Hundreds of protesters in front of a McDonald's may or may not make the local evening news, but a relatively modest national TV campaign (for example, twelve spots costing $2,500 each on CNN's *Headline News*), pointing out that a Big Mac contains over 50 percent fat, can strike to the heart of the fast-food industry. A cheeky anticar spot, aired repeatedly during international Indy and Nascar broadcasts, can begin to unnerve the global automakers. An uncommercial that fingers the global economy as a doomsday machine, aired during the weeks leading up to a G-7 summit meeting, can trigger a worldwide debate about unsustainable overconsumption by the affluent "First" nations of the world.

Eventually, we will have access to the airwaves. We will have the "right to communicate" with each other in a free information environment. In the meantime, TV jamming is still a win-win strategy: If you are able to buy time and get your ad aired, you win by delivering your message to hundreds of thousands of attentive viewers. If the networks refuse to sell you airtime, you publicize that fact. Now you have a news story (the media are always willing to expose a dirty little secret) that will prompt debate in your community about access to the public airwaves and perhaps draw more attention to your cause than if the networks had simply sold you the airtime in the first place.

The Industrial Pincer

Squirming out from under a big, dysfunctional industry that's controlling some aspect of our lives and setting new agendas in that industry requires more than just a hot TV spot and a little ad hoc anger. Breaking the auto industry's hold on our transportation and environmental policies, or the food industry's hold on our nutritional agendas, or the fashion industry's hold on what constitutes attractiveness requires protracted meme warfare on many fronts over many years. The "pincer strategy" is a way to organize the forces. You apply it as follows:

1. You attack the industry from above with hard-hitting media thrusts. You break its unchallenged run on television by airing dissenting ads. You run subverts and spoofs in magazines. You place anti-ads right next to their ads in the urban landscape.

2. Simultaneously, you attack from below. You lobby at the grassroots level. You contact citizens' groups (cyclists, vegans, women's groups, Christians against TV violence, Green entrepreneurs) and catalyze

actions (anticar rallies, street parties, stickering campaigns, Fashin' Bashin' Weeks, cyberpetitions) calculated to attract press and TV coverage.

3. You apply the pincer to the industry and don't let up for at least two years.

A well-organized pincer will get millions of people thinking about their lives—about eating better, driving less, jumping off the fashion treadmill, downshifting. Eventually, the national mood will evolve. Single-occupant commuters will begin to resemble the smokers of today—outsiders, even villains. People scarfing a Big Mac, Coke and fries for lunch will feel a little guilty, a little sick, a little stupid. Teenagers wearing Nike caps and Calvin Klein jeans won't feel so trendy anymore.

That's when these industries will change. That's when the global automakers will suddenly realize there's no future in single-occupant commuting. When McDonald's stops trying to sell another generation on a deep-fried, high-fat diet. When the beauty myth loses its hold. That's when the corporate cool machine suddenly starts spluttering, and, in a great surge of self-determination, we the people stand up and reclaim our culture.

In my more melodramatic moments over the last ten years, I have let myself imagine the culture-jamming crusade building to a single, almost solemn moment of reckoning, like the scene in Shakespeare's *Henry V* where the king summons his troops before the battle of Agincourt and delivers the gut-check talk:

> *And gentlemen in England now a-bed*
> *Shall think themselves accursed they were not here*
> *And hold their manhoods cheap whiles any speaks*
> *That fought with us upon Saint Crispin's day.*

It's not inconceivable that the culture-jamming movement will be remembered by our grandchildren for having been one of the catalysts of the great planetary transformation that shook the world in the early years of the new millennium. By that time, the neoclassical-economics spell will have been broken, and the fight to wrest sovereign power from corporations will be largely won. The freedom and cultural empowerment our grandkids enjoy will be the one we fought for, and won. "What did you do?" they will ask us. "Were you there when Philip Morris Inc. bit the dust? When the True-Cost Party of America won the election? When the 'right to communicate' was enshrined in the Universal Declaration of Human Rights?"

And then, like King Henry, we will strip our sleeves and show our scars.

summer

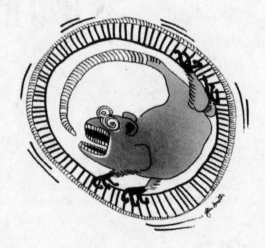

RAGE

Rage—call it wrath, if you like, or righteous anger—is good. When it wells up suddenly from deep inside you, it's immediate, compelling, real. It's the only emotion strong enough to start a war or (think Vietnam protests) stop one. When it springs from personal frustration, rage brings about low-level justice. It gets the boiler in your building fixed, the loud upstairs neighbor evicted, the reckless driver fined, your delinquent teenage daughter grounded. When it springs from a sense of moral affront, it brings profound change. It stops cosmetics testing on animals, toughens juvenile crime laws, improves working conditions on factory floors and topples governments.

Rage drives revolutions.

It used to be easier to work up a good rage. It used to be easy to figure out whom you were raging at, even if that was everyone and everything. ("What're you rebelling against?" they asked the young Marlon Brando. "Whadd'ya got?" he replied.) These days there are fewer obvious lightning rods for rage, fewer out-and-out villains. The people you're most inclined to get roaring mad at—sales clerks, phone solicitors, loan officers—are often just front-line agents in a corporate megasystem. It's the system, not its agents, that is the problem. Trying to get personal with a system is like trying to get personal with a broken toaster. You just end up feeling stupid, because your rage makes no difference at all.

The overarching "system" these days is consumer capitalism, which since World War II, Americans have understood to be the solution to the country's woes, not the source of them. Capitalism has always been sold to us as our ticket to freedom, the antidote to the hellish bureaucracy of communism. But consumer capitalism—the society of spectacle—can be an even more insidious form of social control than communism, which is simply paternalism run amok. Communism is blunt and obvious, like a blow with a club. Capitalism's consumer culture cannibalizes your spirit over time, it puts you to work as an obedient "slave component" of the system without your ever even knowing it.

Imagine you're flaked out on the couch watching TV. You're very relaxed, the way a hypnotized patient is relaxed. Gradually, you feel your energy, or at least your desire to do anything but continue to watch, draining away. You are warm and insensate. But as drug experiences go, this is less than blissful. After a few hours you know something is wrong. You want to get up, but can't. You think you might be going crazy. Someone is doing this to you. Someone is sucking you dry. But who? The guy who owns the network (Michael Eisner)? The guy who dreams up this dreck (Aaron Spelling)? The doofus who delivers it (David Hasselhoff)? Or do you blame yourself? *You're* complicit—tuning in, keeping the numbers up, feeding the machine. What we have here is a kind of diffusion of responsibility. It's the same phenomenon that allows soldiers in wartime to rationalize away any self-blame for the atrocities going on around them. Being a tiny gear in a vast engine of responsibility gets you off the hook. If everyone's a villain—if we are all caught in the media-consumer trance—then no one is to blame. It's hard to generate any good, focused anger in these circumstances, but it's very, very easy to get depressed.

Bit by bit since the '50s, the spectacle has swallowed us up. We don't trust the reality of our desires anymore. We've grown cynical and afraid. We've forgotten what it feels like to get angry — how to *do* rage. We listen to that ultraconservative part of our brain that says: Hold back, be reasonable, things aren't so bad. We've lost touch with our inner Peter Finch, the part of ourselves that throws open the window and screams into the street, "I'm mad as hell and I'm not going to take it anymore!" Instead, we lie in front of our TVs like beaten dogs. We toady to corporations and wear their brand logos like serfs. We breathe bad air, drink foul water, lick corporate lollipops and never let out a peep.

Why are we so docile and obedient? Is it because there's just not as much to fight for? Hardly. There has never been more at stake. The fate of the planet hangs in the balance. Never in human history has so much defiance been needed from so many. But for some strange reason we deny our anger and sit tight.

Postmodern cynicism is rage that can no longer get it up. It is powerlessness, disconnection and shame. It's the loneliest kind of rage there is, different from the kinds of rage we've known in the past, which were born of injustice and nurtured by a clearly identifiable enemy. Postmodern rage is a volatile mix of strong feelings long suppressed: one part "eco-rage," an appalled disbelief at the way human beings are blithely destroying the natural world, and one part a profound, information-age anger I call "psycho-rage." You may not have had a name for this particular emotion until now, but you know if you have it. You're bored, yet anxious. Your moods soar and dive. Barely controllable anger wells up without warning out of nowhere.

Psycho-rage spikes when you realize you're trapped in a carnival of staged events: corporate America's idea of fun. It intensifies with every hour you spend in front of the TV watching the endless parade of dramatized home invasions, boxing bouts, space-shuttle launches, election debates, stock-market analyses, celebrity gossip and genocidal wars— interrupted every few minutes by ads for cars and cosmetics and holidays in Hawaii. It reaches a crescendo as you realize (too late) that ever since you were a baby crawling around that TV set, you've been propa-

THE PRODUCT IS YOU
15-SECOND TV SPOT

The camera moves slowly toward a young man watching TV in his living room.

Voice:
"Your living room
is the factory . . .

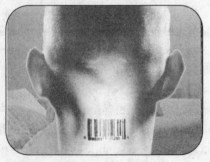

. . . the product being
manufactured is *you*."

MEME WARFARE TONIGHT 1-800-663-1243

gandized and suckered, your neurons pickled in erotica, violence and marketing hype. You have become less than what you once were. The forces of nurture and genetics that make you a unique human being have met equal and opposing forces trying to reduce you to an obedient consumer. You have joined the North American consumer cult of the insatiables. In Buddhist terminology, you have become a "hungry ghost," with an enormous belly and pinhole-size mouth. And you will never be truly "full" again.

The strange thing is, you don't really mind. In fact, on some level, you're happy as a clam. You find yourself actually enjoying the ride, savoring the spectacle. Your daily dose of circus sound-and-light dissolves under your tongue. You can't stop watching as the bombs land on Baghdad. Your tears flow freely for Princess Di. You can't get enough news about President Clinton's escapades. You press the remote and the show goes on.

Once in a while, in a flash of insight, you understand that something is terribly, terribly wrong with your life, and that a rude and barren future awaits unless you leap up off the couch *right now*.

Then the moment passes. Your opening came and you didn't move. You couldn't muster the clarity of mind to figure out what to do, let alone the energy to do it.

And so your rage remains underground.

Rage is a signal like pain or lust. If you learn to trust it and ride shotgun on it, watching it without suppressing it, you gain power and lose cynicism. "Lying is the major form of human stress," the American psychologist Brad Blanton once said, and to the extent that failure to acknowledge your rage is really just lying to yourself, then jamming a coin into a monopoly newspaper box or liberating a billboard in the middle of the night can be a rather honest and joyful thing to do.

There's an anger, a rage-driven defiance, that is healthy, ethical and empowering. It contains the conviction that *change is possible*—both for you and for your antagonist. Learning how to jam our culture with this rage may be one of the few ways left to feel truly among the quick in the Huxleyan mindscape of new millennium capitalism.

THE SECOND AMERICAN REVOLUTION

(An Assertiveness Training Workshop for Culture Jammers)

Think of the history of the United States as a play in four acts. In the first act, America is a puppet nation, its early settlers controlled from afar by their British masters. In the second act, the Americans rise up. A great revolution brings power to the people and they set up a new, more democratic way of governing themselves that inspires the world. In the long and tragic third act, now in its dramatic finale, America is stricken with consumption and begins to die. Overwhelmed by corporate spectacle and power, the once proud democracy devolves into a corporate state. The people grow decadent and forget how to be free.

Now the fourth act is about to begin. It is an act of reversal, recovery, redemption. The American people experience a great awakening. Systematically, they undertake to dismantle their corporate state and recover the sovereignty that has been lost over the last century. "Sovereign people do not beg of, or negotiate with subordinate entities which we created—sovereign people *instruct* subordinate entities," says Richard Grossman, codirector of the Program on Cor-

porations, Law and Democracy, one of the architects of this grand
new shift. "When a subordinate entity violates the terms of its creation, and undermines our ability to govern ourselves, we are required
to move in swiftly and accountably to cut this cancer out of the body
politic."

Act Four of the story of America is about breaking the media-
consumer trance. It's about taking the ™ out of America™. It's about
putting corporations back in the box and revoking many of the constitutional rights we have granted them over the past two hundred years.
It's about calling these subordinate entities to heel.

The goal of this workshop is to spark a dramatic personal mindshift that will change the way you relate to corporations. Once you've
experienced this shift, you'll feel ashamed for having been so docile and
subservient for so long. Your days will be charged with a new sense of
autonomy and mission. You'll derive immense pleasure from tussling
with corporations, putting them in their place. You'll train yourself to
always take the position of power, to be mindful of the fact that *you* are
a human being and the corporation is merely a legal construct your
species thought up.

By the end of this section, you'll have developed skills to take
back the freedom and dignity that are rightfully yours. The mindshift
will happen gradually. Corporate agendas are so deeply woven into
our lives that it's hard to see them, much less jam them (we take corporate power and privilege for granted in the same way the power and
privilege of royalty were taken for granted a hundred years ago). It's a
slow detox.

You will begin with simple acts of resistance, but in the end you
will change utterly the way you see your place in consumer culture.

In each of the following scenarios, you have two broad options:
You can roll over and squeal like a pig—i.e., act the way corporations
want you to act—or you can seize control of the situation—*détourn*
it—and start acting like an empowered sovereign citizen. But as we will
see, there are degrees of sovereignty. Some paths to freedom are more
direct than others.

Drop Your Facade of Politeness

The telephone company sends you your monthly statement. You see it has made a mistake and overcharged you. You call and explain your problem to an operator. "OK, no problem, we can fix this," she says. "Please mail or fax the bill back to us with a little note explaining the problem, and we'll take care of it."

You can do as she asks. That's what most people do. It avoids a lot of trouble and lets you get on with your day. It also means following an arrogant corporate procedure designed to save them time and money at your expense.

Here's the sovereign path. Drop your facade of politeness and say, "Listen, this is your mistake, so instead of *me* sending the bill back to you, why don't *you* send me a new bill with the adjusted amount and then I'll pay it." Insist on *your* procedure, and be prepared to immediately switch servers if she refuses to go along.

In a similar vein, I know a woman who, whenever she receives an unsolicited fax on her home fax line, replies by faxing back a jet-black sheet of paper (which drains the memory and the toner of the machine at the other end). She leaves only a tiny window of white that contains this message: "Don't fax me at home again."

Learn to Détourn

It's Monday evening. The phone rings. On the line is a woman who works for a major insurance company. Would you be interested in receiving information about the term life plan which she understands, by her records, may suit you, given your lifestyle and income level? She is quite aggressive and clearly reading off a card.

Here your options are limited only by your imagination and mood of the moment. You can listen to her spiel and then politely say no. Or you can take the easy way out and lie ("We already have life insurance" or, "I'm sorry, there's no one here by that name"). Or you can get real. "All right, I'll talk to you," you might say, "but only if you stop reading from that card and start speaking to me like a human being." If you're feeling sparky, you could engage her in a conversation about why she took this telemarketing job in the first place and try to talk her into changing jobs. Or you can tell her, truthfully, that you're busy right now, but if you can have her home phone number you'll call her back tonight. (When she refuses, simply say: "You called *me* at home, so why can't I call *you* at home?") Or you can turn the tables on her by saying: "OK, before we go any further you should know that I bill my time out at twenty dollars an hour, with a fifteen-minute minimum, so if you want to talk to me, it's going to cost your company at least five dollars. The meter's running. It's your decision." That's a nifty *détournement*. Once enough people start *détourning* corporate telemarketing thrusts like that, it won't be so cost-effective for them to keep badgering us in our homes.

Clear a Path for Others

One of your checks bounces. You're sure you had enough in the account to cover it. You call up your local bank branch, the one you've been dealing with for twenty years, to find out what happened. This time your call is rerouted to a new 1-800 headquarters at the other end of the country. You ask to speak to someone you know in your local branch. Sorry, not possible, the operator says: All inquiries are now handled from this new office—a cost-cutting move. But this new office doesn't have a history with you, you argue. As of now, the operator tells you, your history begins anew.

Again, you can take the "easy" route and just deal politely with this new person. It would mean caving in, but you're not in the mood for an argument and besides, how can you ever win a fight with a bank?

Consider the cost, though, of not taking this bank on. Every time you capitulate to a corporation, you're letting down everyone who follows you on the path. If you fail to take out a bully or reprogram a bully, the bully is free to bully again.

It's the little daily capitulations we unthinkingly allow, the lumps we swallow without comment, that have landed us in the sorry state of subservience we're in. Every time we lump it we lose a little of our freedom and dignity. A lot of people who habitually give up often say, "Hey, it's not my battle." Or, "What possible difference can I make?" It's this attitude that allows corporations to gain the upper hand in any policy or procedure they decide to foist upon us. The real lesson here is that no fight is too small. Little capitulations inevitably lead to bigger ones, while little victories lead to greater triumphs.

The way we handle daily aggravations places us on a continuum of commitment. At one end of the continuum are little tussles on the phone and in the bank, and at the other end are critical choices about genetic engineering, trade rules and global warming. How we respond personally to the small things determines to a great extent how we respond collectively to the big things. Our everyday life is where the revolution unfolds. That's where the real guerrilla actions take place, and where Marshall McLuhan's World War III will eventually be won or lost.

Learn to Confront

You're recruited by the university hockey team and discover that everyone on the squad is required to wear a jersey with a big swoosh on the front. The uniform is mandatory. This is a "Nike" university (meaning Nike has forked over a lot of money and gear in return for blanket allegiance on campus).

Of course, it's easiest just to wear the damn swoosh and play. The option at the other extreme is to have a blowup with the coach and quit the team in protest.

But here's the jammer's jig. You have a little private chat with each one of your teammates, and then call a meeting. Argue that it's degrading for hockey players to be reduced to human billboards. Then up the ante. Paste posters. Write a story for the campus newspaper. Talk on campus radio. Pull off a wild, attention-grabbing prank. Then demand an audience with the university dean and faculty heads to explain your position. Tell them there will be hell to pay if they don't stop mixing education with marketing.

By getting in the face of corporate America in this way, you're not just being confrontational, you're *demarketing your life*, creating your own choices and learning a whole new strategy of self-reliance. Bit by bit, you wean yourself off name brands, switch your bank account to the local credit union, buy what you need at locally owned stores, supplement the news you usually get with alternative sources. You learn to reward the good with your dollars and your time, and punish the bad by refusing to buy in. You develop new habits and routines, a new attitude that becomes engrained. You never allow a corporate rep who says "I'm sorry, but that's company policy, sir" off the hook. Instead, you confront her and wrestle her down on the spot. If she hangs tough, you ask to see her boss. If he hangs tough, you go over his head. You take names, make notes, stay cool. You never let a corporation forget who is serving whom.

Corporations have a lot of experience with (and a "procedure" for) dealing with troublemakers like you. Decide in advance how much you're prepared to risk. Don't pick a fight if you don't have the time to see it through. Preplan confrontations. Decide how far you're willing to go and what your final move will be if your ride up the company hierarchy hits a dead end. Are you ready to close your account at the bank? Cancel an order? Create a public scene? Engage in civil disobedience? Take legal action? Or will you settle for an appointment with the manager next week?

As you make more and more committed choices, you will feel more alive, free, real. Bit by bit, you'll also start winning more tussles than you lose, and you'll discover the joy of jamming: that great, exhilarating power for change that every human being has.

Reframe Debates

You've decided to take the step from personal to collective action. Disgusted with ongoing fast-food imperialism, you decide to join a sidewalk protest at the local McDonald's.

WHY ARE YOU BUYING YOUR FOOD FROM A TOBACCO COMPANY?

Did you know that every product pictured here is owned by Philip Morris, the world's largest cigarette company? Chances are you've been helping to promote Marlboro cigarettes without even knowing it. Now you can withdraw that support by personally boycotting these products. It's like giving money to a health organization that's working to find a cure for cancer—but in this case, you're taking money away from a corporation that causes it. So next time you're at the supermarket—try it. You'll like it.

Normally, these kinds of events follow a standard script. Protesters distribute leaflets critical of the way the corporation promotes poor nutrition and scalps the South American rain forest for pastureland. The whole protest ritual is preframed. On one side is McDonald's, the established and popular multibillion-dollar enterprise. On the other side is a bunch of scruffy, long-haired reactionaries with their tired, Lefty grievances. The protest leaders deliberately defy the police and are arrested. Reporters show up and get a few angry quotes. A news story finds its way into the city section of the local paper or maybe makes the evening news. But nothing changes. McDonald's continues to open as many new outlets as it wants, continues to hook kids via Saturday morning cartoons, continues to spend a billion and a half dollars a year worldwide on advertising, and continues in large part to set the planet's nutritional agenda.

You could propose another way to organize your protest. This time, your group walks around the restaurant in an orderly fashion. You don't encroach on McDonald's private property. The police have no legal reason to arrest you.

When a reporter asks, "What are you protesting against, exactly?" you answer: "Please, let's get something straight right off the top. We're not protesters. We're *citizens* of this city concerned about the way McDonald's is marketing fast food to our children. We want to have some say in how many fast-food restaurants there are in our neighborhoods and what license fees they should be paying to city hall for that privilege."

Wow! Suddenly, the issue is reframed. Suddenly, this isn't a bunch of anti-McDonald's protesters; it's a group of citizens asserting their right to decide what happens in their city. The citizens are once again the natives, the landowners, the original settlers, and it's their rights that are being infringed on, not the corporation's.

The reporter who had practically written her story in advance (" . . . insert inflammatory quote from protester here . . . ") now has that word "protester" yanked out from under her. She will write her piece differently now. Her ritual has been interrupted because a smart jammer reframed the debate.

And the next day a citizen will read the paper and say, "Yes, that makes sense to me. There *are* too many fast-food joints around here. I like the idea of regulating how many of them can operate in my neighborhood. And fast-food franchises like McDonald's should pay bigger license fees to city hall. Maybe we should charge them fifty thousand dollars per year, or even more. We should be able to do that if we want to. It's *our* neighborhood. It's *our* city. And now that I think about it, maybe we don't need so much fast-food advertising on kids' TV shows either."

Reframing an issue is as simple as figuring out what the core issues are. Gandhi redefined the conflict in colonial India. "The function of a civil resistance is to provoke response," he told his people, "and we will continue to provoke until they respond or they change the law." The strength of reframing in this way was that "the resisters" became the active agents and the British government became the reactive agents. The power dynamic was inverted. From then on it was the resisters who set the agenda.

Maintain Your Sovereignty

In the Pacific Northwest, a handful of forestry giants, granted power to "manage" the resource, have a long history of committing all manner of ecological crimes, from cutting at unsustainable rates to clear-cutting in watersheds. Their legacy is a barren landscape of stumps and muddy, dying salmon streams.

For more than twenty years the environmental lobby has fought back. Groups like Greenpeace, the Sierra Club and the Western Canada Wilderness Committee have issued thousands of press releases detailing the various harms the forest companies have done. Ecoguides have taken thousands of visitors to see the ancient virgin forests (making them aware, in the most personal way, of what's at stake in the woods). Volunteers have built boardwalks under the forests' cathedrallike canopies. Over the years, hundreds of passionate protesters have been arrested for blocking logging roads or chaining themselves to the loggers' equipment.

Environmentalists have won many concessions. Tracts of rain forest have been spared by government edict. Parks have been created. Clear-cutting practices have been changed.

Yet the fundamental problems remain. The forest companies are still cutting above sustainable levels, still trashing the salmon runs, still leaving a bunch of mismanaged tree farms for future generations to deal with. And when the protests get too heavy, when the business climate is no longer conducive, when the lucrative old-growth forests are gone, the logging companies will move their operations to Indonesia or Brazil or some other place where the pickings are better.

"How much harm does a company have to do before we question its right to exist?" asked the author of *The Ecology of Commerce*, Paul Hawken. With that question, he reframed the whole corporate debate. Try it; it's empowering. Instead of contesting the harms one by one, instead of asking the logging company to stop doing bad things here and here and here, start questioning their legitimacy, their legal right to continue conducting business in your state or province.

Reframing an issue so that *you*, not a corporation, are the sovereign entity is a little like looking at those Gestalt drawings in psychology class: Is it a goblet or is it two faces nose to nose? Once the perceptual shift has occurred and you see the faces, the goblet disappears.

To get an idea of what the shift feels like on an emotional level, think of your relationship with your father or mother. Recall the many little scraps you've had over the years. Then think back to that moment when, in some not-quite-precisely-defined way, the power dynamic suddenly changed. It probably happened when you were in your mid-teens. Maybe your father grounded you for a bit too long, or lectured you a bit too loudly, or otherwise went a bit too far in asserting his authority. And something inside you snapped. You looked into his eyes and instead of seeing strength, confidence and certitude, you suddenly saw insecurity, confusion and fear. For the first time in your life, you talked back at him, even if that meant storming out of the house and living somewhere else for a while, even if it meant reducing your mom to tears, even if it meant raising your fist. In the past all that would have been unthinkable, but the world had suddenly changed. That day, for the first time, you became your own person and nobody—not even your father—was going to push you around.

A teenager's declaration of independence is one of the universal rites of passage. What the world needs now is a similar rite of triumphant passage for citizens in the corporate house.

Fifty years ago, Alabama blacks sat in the backs of buses and at their own end of the lunch counter without thinking twice about it. Many women once believed they didn't deserve to vote. When I was a teenager, women were discouraged from driving a car because, hey, everyone knew they were terrible drivers. And many women believed it was true. They smiled and joked about it and let the men do the driving.

Today, we're caught in the same kind of reflexive subservience to corporations. We think it's normal for them to have more rights than we do. We think it's proper for them to set the rules of doing business in our communities. We think it's legitimate for them to clear-cut ancient forests, influence elections, run our airwaves, take politicians on jaunts to the Bahamas and draft the world trade rules.

But it isn't, and once you've reframed the issues of sovereignty, power and privilege, you'll wonder why you ever thought it was.

Now, having completed this workshop and adjusted your personal mind-set, you may be ready to go to the next level—to actually tinker with the corporate genetic code.

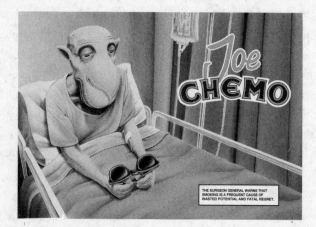

GROUNDING THE CORPORATION

A corporation has no heart, no soul, no morals. It cannot feel pain. You cannot argue with it. That's because a corporation is not a living thing, but a process—an efficient way of generating revenue. It takes energy from outside (capital, labor, raw materials) and transforms it in various ways. In order to continue "living" it needs to meet only one condition: Its income must equal its expenditures over the long term. As long as it does that, it can exist indefinitely.

When a corporation hurts people or damages the environment, it will feel no sorrow or remorse because it is *intrinsically unable to do so*. (It may sometimes apologize, but that's not remorse—that's public relations.) Buddhist scholar David Loy, of Tokyo's Bunkyo University, put it this way: "A corporation cannot laugh or cry; it cannot enjoy the world or suffer with it. Most of all a corporation cannot *love*." That's because corporations are legal fictions. Their "bodies" are just judicial constructs, and that, according to Loy, is why they are so dangerous. "They are essentially ungrounded to the earth and its creatures, to the pleasures and responsibilities that derive from being manifestations of the earth." Corporations are in the most literal and chilling sense "dispassionate."

We demonize corporations for their unwavering pursuit of growth, power and wealth. Yet, let's face it: They are simply carrying out genetic orders. That's exactly what corporations were designed—by us—to do. Trying to rehabilitate a corporation, urging it to behave responsibly, is a fool's game. The only way to change the behavior of a corporation is to recode it; rewrite its charter; reprogram it.

When a corporation like General Electric, Exxon, Union Carbide or Philip Morris breaks the law, causes an environmental catastrophe or otherwise undermines the public interest, the usual result is that . . . nothing very much happens. The corporation may be forced to pay a fine, revamp its safety procedures, face a boycott. At worst—and this is very rare—it is forced into bankruptcy. The shareholders lose money and the employees lose their jobs. Usually, though, the shareholders move on to other investments, and company executives find work elsewhere. In fact, it's often the public and low-level employees who suffer the most when a corporation dies.

What if there was another, more serious, potential outcome, one that would lay responsibility where it belongs? What if each shareholder was deemed personally responsible and liable for collateral damage to bystanders or harms to the environment? Why shouldn't it be so? If you're a shareholder, a part-owner of a corporation, and you reap the rewards when the going is good, why shouldn't you be held responsible for that company when it becomes criminally liable?

If we rewrote the rules of incorporation so that every shareholder assumed partial liability, financial markets would immediately undergo dramatic change. Fewer shares would be traded. Instead of simply choosing the biggest cash cows, potential shareholders would carefully investigate the backgrounds of the companies they were about to sink their money into. They would think twice about buying shares in Philip Morris Inc. or R. J. Reynolds or Monsanto. Too risky. They would choose resource companies with good environmental records. They would stay away from multinationals that use child workers or break labor laws overseas. In other words, *the shareholders would be grounded*—forced to care and take responsibility. Stock markets would cease to be gambling casinos. Our whole business culture would heave.

We made an enormous mistake when we let shareholders off the legal-liability hook. But it's not too late to rectify that mistake. We, the people, created the corporate charter and the rules for buying stocks and shares, and now, we the people must change those rules.

The same approach can be extended to corporate crime. When a human being commits a major crime—gets caught trafficking cocaine or robbing a store—society metes out harsh justice. The felon automatically loses his political rights (to vote and hold office) and if the crime is serious enough, he does hard time. When he gets out of jail he's marked for life. Employers won't hire him. People who know his background won't trust him. He can't travel freely across borders. In some parts of America, if he commits three felonies, he's put away for life.

Compare that to the worst that might happen to a corporation caught flagrantly breaking the law. The public is outraged. The CEO loses his job. There's a shake-up in the boardroom. The company faces a class-action suit and pays out a lot of money. But . . . at the end of the day, the executives of a criminal corporation really don't have so much to worry about. Their chances of ending up in jail are next to zero. And the corporation itself loses none of its political or legal rights to continue to do business, lobby Congress or participate in elections. In the end, the corporation hires a new CEO, settles the suit, launches a PR campaign to regain public confidence. This is often seen as just the price of doing business. That's why the executives of rogue corporations like Philip Morris can keep lying to us, hiding information and otherwise flouting the law with impunity year after year after year. There is no penalty they fear.

We must find ways to instill that fear. We must enact tough new corporate criminal liability laws. Repeat offenders should be barred for a specified number of years from selling things to the government. They should be ineligible to hold government contracts and licenses for television stations. They should not be allowed to finance political campaigns or lobby Congress, and they should forfeit their legal rights just as individual criminals do.

We must rewrite the rules of incorporation in such a way that any company caught repeatedly and willfully dumping toxic wastes; damaging watersheds; violating antipollution laws; harming employees, customers, or the people living near its factories; engaging in price fixing; defrauding its customers; or keeping vital information secret *automatically* has its charter revoked, its assets sold off and the money funneled into a superfund for its victims.

There are precedents for this kind of action, though you have to go back a century to find them. In 1884, the people of New York City, citing a willful pattern of abuse, asked their attorney general to revoke the charter of the Standard Oil Trust of New York (they succeeded). The state of Pennsylvania revoked the charters of a number of banks that were found to be operating against the public interest. Michigan, Ohio and New York revoked the charters of oil, sugar and whiskey trusts. In 1890, the highest court in New York State revoked the charter of the North River Sugar Refining Corporation with these words: "The judgment sought against the defendant is one of corporate death. The state, which created, asks us to destroy, and the penalty invoked represents the extreme rigor of the law. The life of a corporation is, indeed, less than that of the humblest citizen. . . . "

Warnings about corporate consolidation have also come out of more recent court decisions. In 1976, U.S. Supreme Court Justices White, Brennan and Marshall noted that "the special status of corporations has placed them in a position to control a vast amount of economic power by which they may, if not regulated, dominate not only the economy but also the very heart of our democracy, the electoral process."

Today, after one hundred years of inaction, corporate charters are once again being challenged.

In May 1998, New York Attorney General Dennis Vacco revoked the charters of the Council for Tobacco Research and the Tobacco Institute, on the grounds that they are tobacco-funded fronts that serve "as propaganda arms of the industry."

In Alabama, the only state in the union where a private citizen can file a legal petition to dissolve a corporation, Judge William Wynn did just that. In June 1998, acting as a private citizen (and comparing his actions to making a citizen's arrest), Wynn named five tobacco companies that, he asserted, have broken state child-abuse laws and should be shut down. "The grease has been hot for a year now, and it's time to put the chicken in," he said.

On September 10, 1998, in what may be the largest corporate charter revocation effort in a century, thirty individuals and organizations (including the National Organization for Women, Rainforest Action Network and National Lawyers Guild) petitioned California Attorney General Dan Lungren to pull the plug on Unocal Corporation, which, they claim, engages in environmental devastation, unethical treatment of workers and gross human-rights violations.

And on Tuesday, November 3, 1998, in the fiercely political university town of Arcata, California, citizens, in the first ballot initiative of its kind in U.S. history, voted 3,139 to 2,056 to "ensure democratic control of all corporations conducting business within the city." Now, in town hall meetings and an ongoing citywide conversation, the people of Arcata will decide what role they want corporations to play in their community.

The 1886 *Santa Clara County* v. *Southern Pacific Railroad* Supreme Court decision declared that corporations were "natural persons" under the U.S. Constitution. Suddenly, corporations "came to life" among us, and started enjoying the same rights and freedoms as we, the citizens who created them. One of the ultimate long-term strategies for jammers is to revisit that judgment, have it overturned, and ensure that the corporate "I" will never again rise up in our society.

It will be a long and vicious battle for the soul of America and the outcome is far from clear. In the next century, will America evolve toward a radical democracy or an even more entrenched corporate state? Will more and more of the world economy be "centrally planned by global megacorporations"? Will we live and work on Planet Earth, or Planet Inc.? The only way to avoid this latter, nightmare scenario is for a few million Americans to start thinking and acting like empowered, sovereign citizens.

PETITION

To Revoke Philip Morris's Corporate Charter
in the State of New York

Dear Attorney General Eliot L. Spitzer:

We, the undersigned citizens of the United States and New York, who are sovereign over government and corporations, have the responsibility of keeping both these institutions subservient.
In May of 1998, The Council for Tobacco Research USA Inc. and The Tobacco Institute Inc. were placed in receivership as a direct result of a petition your predecessor Dennis Vacco initiated against these two groups for serving as "propaganda arms" of tobacco companies.
Now we ask you to initiate similar proceedings against Philip Morris, Inc.

According to New York State law, you, the attorney general, may bring an action for the dissolution of a corporation upon one or more of the following grounds:

That the corporation has exceeded the authority conferred upon it by law, or has violated any provision of law whereby it has forfeited its charter, or carried on, conducted, or transacted its business in a persistently fraudulent or illegal manner.

For over 25 years Philip Morris, Inc., has transacted its business in a persistently fraudulent manner and therefore we the undersigned call upon you to commence proceedings to dissolve the corporate existence of Philip Morris, Inc.

name	address	signature

Please sign, photocopy and return this petition to the Media Foundation, 1243 W. 7th Ave, Vancouver, BC, V6H 1B7, Canada.
Or fax it to: 604-737-6021. Or find out more and sign the cyberpetition at <www.adbusters.org>

One way to jump-start this "second American revolution" is to make an example of one of the world's biggest corporate criminals—Philip Morris Inc. Launch a TV campaign that tells the horrifying truth about that company's long criminal record. Organize a massive boycott of its food products, collect a mind-addling number of petition signatures, keep applying the pressure and simply never let up until the attorney general of the state of New York revokes the company's charter.

THE EVOLUTION OF MARKETING

Marketing: selling society on
an ever-expanding horizon of
products and services.

↓

Social Marketing: selling society
on a new set of ideas, lifestyles,
philosophies and worldviews.

↓

Negamarketing: urging society to
consume less electricity,
gasoline, energy, materials.

↓

Demarketing: unselling the consumer
society; turning the incredible
power of marketing against itself.

DEMARKETING LOOPS

Midtown Manhattan, 1999: In the boardroom of a famous lifestyle magazine, a young editor leans forward, removes his Gauthier glasses and broaches a Big Idea.

"Two words: 'Demarketing Chic.' "

By the expressions of his colleagues, he can tell he's halfway there. They like it. They may love it.

"Here's the deal," he explains. "The world has gotten just unbelievably commercial, right? And people are starting to go a little crazy from it. They've completely bought into it, and it's been a hell of a ride, but now they're reaching a saturation point. They think maybe they're getting to the end of this business of glitz and hype and Ya Gotta Have It. So we say, in effect, Yeah. Your instincts are right. For the first time in forever, marketing isn't cool. Excess isn't cool."

He takes a slug of Pellegrino and continues.

"We do a trend piece—not a think piece but more of a package. Four or five spreads. Maybe we devote a whole issue to it. We really sell the idea hard."

"And we do that by . . ."

"By rounding up the least commercial people you can think of. People who stand in opposition to the whole idea of conspicuous consumerism. Anticonsumers. Icons of simplicity. We build the package around these people. We turn them into stars."

"Right . . ."

"So, for example, the Quaker on the side of the oatmeal box. We find the actual Quaker who posed for that picture and we do a Q-and-A thing."

"The actual Quaker?"

"Well, some actor who we say is the actual Quaker."

"Okay, good. Who else?"

"Sister Wendy."

"The art-critic nun?"

"Yeah. Very, very cool, in her way. We get her to hang out with Cy Twombly and Julian Schnabel. Just shoot the breeze with these guys. At Schnabel's place, by the pool."

"More."

"The Dalai Lama—a very funny guy, apparently—headlining on amateur night at The Comedy Store in L.A."

"More."

"Mother Teresa."

"Too late. More."

"'Those Crafty Amish' on The Learning Channel."

"More."

"Ralph Nader in a Martha Stewart–style shoot at Walden Pond, in front of Thoreau's cabin."

"Can we find Thoreau's old cabin?"

"Doesn't matter. We'll build another. No one will know."

Demarketing. The whole concept lends itself to satire, possibly because it seems so foreign to most of us. The word has a sinister ring to it. Whatever else demarketing is, it's certainly un-American.

Advertising and marketing are so deeply embedded in our culture now that it's hard to imagine a time when product placement and network logo "burns" and "bugs" weren't everywhere you looked, when our lifestyles and culture weren't predicated on consumption. But that pre-marketing era was not so long ago: only two generations. Demarketing is about restoring a little of the sanity we enjoyed back then. It's about uncooling our consumer culture, reclaiming the real, recovering some of what has been lost since consumerism became the First World's new religion.

The other day, in a moment of guy-to-guy candor, a friend challenged me on my demarketing philosophy and my whole outlook on life. "Kalle," he said, "you complain about advertising, you complain about the big, bad media, you bitch about how much we consume and how we govern ourselves and how corporations are ruining America. You say you want a radically different way of life—a revolution. But would you really want to live in the kind of world you're proposing?"

I asked him to be more specific.

"Isn't the live-fast, die-hard lifestyle you can't stand the very thing that makes it so much fun to be American? Living large is our inheritance. It's what we fought for and won. We have the highest standard of living in the world because we earned it. We did it by taking risks and being inventive and working our butts off. So now maybe I want to drive fast, and rattle the windows with my music, and have sex with my wife in our backyard swimming pool, and watch *Monday Night Football* while burgers grill on the barbecue. And I want to be able to do these things without having to listen to your sanctimonious objections."

My friend had just returned from New York, which he sees as an exciting microcosm of America. "Sure it has problems. It's big, it's loud, it's congested, you can step on a dirty needle in Central Park and the cab driver may be too scared to take you to Harlem. But I'll bet if you asked most New Yorkers they'd tell you they wouldn't want to live anywhere else. If you sanitized New York, it wouldn't be New York. It'd be Baltimore. And if you sanitized America, it wouldn't be America. It'd be Sweden or Canada. Life wouldn't be worth living."

"You just don't get it," I told him. "I'm not trying to sanitize America. The world I'm proposing isn't some watered-down, politically correct place. It's wilder and more interesting than your world in every way. It's open TV airwaves where meme wars, not ratings wars, are fought every day. It's radical democracy—people telling governments and corporations what to do instead of the other way around. It's empowered citizens deciding for themselves what's 'cool'—not a society of consumer drones suckling at the corporate teat. It's living a life that's connected to the planet, knowing something about it, caring for it and handing it down to our children in some kind of decent shape.

"What I'm saying is that the American dream isn't working anymore, so let's face that reality and start building a new one."

I noticed my friend roll his eyes a couple of times as I spoke. In many ways he is the typical North American—ambitious, competitive, successful. If he could convince me that he really is happy and alive, I'd have to concede that his way, though it's not my way, is perfectly valid. But I just don't see it. The supersize American lifestyle generates at least a little guilt in every marginally thoughtful person who pursues it. There's a lot of dirty laundry in my friend's life that he can't ignore, no matter how far under the bed he shoves it. He sees me as a disgruntled Lefty pissing on the American parade; I see him as a man in upper-income-bracket denial, getting what he can while the going is good even as his world is collapsing around him. Of one thing I am sure: His hyperconsumptive lifestyle isn't cool anymore. The old American dream is dying. Change is coming.

One of the great secrets of demarketing the American dream is *détourning* it, in the public imagination, with a dream that's even more seductive. What's better than being rich? *Being spontaneous, authentic, alive.*

The new American dream is simply to approach life full-on, without undue fear or crippling self-censorship, pursuing joy and novelty as if tomorrow you'll be in the ground. The Situationists called this impulse "the will to playful creation," and they believed it should be extended "to all known forms of human relationships." There's no one more alive than the person who is openly, freely improvising—which is why the best stand-up comics love hecklers, and why the best hosts love wild-card dinner guests, and why the most electric political figures love deviating from their prepared scripts on live TV. There's no other way to discover what's at your core. This is what the new American dream is all about, and this is the kind of person the culture jammer aspires to be: someone who, to paraphrase Ray Bradbury, "jumps off cliffs and builds his wings on the way down."

Uncooling Consumption

On the most basic level, demarketing is simply about not buying. An anticonsumerist lifestyle flat-out repudiates the whole idea of marketing. When you don't buy, you don't buy in to consumer culture. When you don't buy in, corporations lose their hold on you.

One increasingly visible group of people have embraced this idea as a faith. They have looked hard at the way we do things in this country and decided it's no longer their way. Somewhere between the time Faith Popcorn coined the term "cashing out" and the time actor Sherry Stringfield walked away from the TV show *E.R.* (to rediscover the true meaning of life, a.k.a. leisure time and her partner), the downshifting movement took off. Thousands of Americans now call their lifestyle "voluntary simplicity" (after Duane Elgin's 1981 book of the same name). Some of these downshifters left high-powered jobs and took drastic pay cuts in order to make more time for family, friends, community, meaningful work. Others were wage slaves who simply decided to improve what Vicki Robin and Joe Dominguez, in *Your Money or Your Life*, call their "joy-to-stuff ratio." Away with frantic living, they have declared. Away with the acquisitive, secular culture that causes even the most sensible souls to drift out of plumb. Too much work, too much clutter, too much distance between expectation and outcome, between investment and payoff, between head and heart will spell the end of us. The downshifters concluded that a higher goal than to amass wealth is to concentrate on culture as Alexander Solzhenitsyn defined it: "the development, enrichment and improvement of non-material life." They understand intuitively what statistics bear out: The aggregate level of

BUY NOTHING DAY
30-SECOND TV SPOT

Voice:
"The average North American consumes five times more than a Mexican . . .

. . . ten times more than a Chinese person and thirty times more than a person in India.

We are the most voracious consumers in the world... a world that could die because of the way we North Americans live.

Give it a rest.
November 26 is
Buy Nothing Day."

MEME WARFARE TONIGHT 1-800-663-1243

American life fulfillment peaked in 1957, and with a couple of brief exceptions, it's been downhill from there.

We hear many dramatic downshifting stories: the eight-figure bond trader who, while getting his shoes shined, picks up a copy of *The Tightwad Gazette* or *Living Green* ("Live simply, that all may simply live"), has an epiphany, bails out of the modern contest and flees to the country to farm hogs or write murder mysteries. But this kind of downshifter is hardly the norm.

Many downshifters had no choice in the matter; they were canned, and that proved to be the best thing that ever happened to them. Alice Kline, whom Juliet Schor describes in *The Overspent American*, was a merchandising director for a high-fashion company. When she was wooed to return to lucrative full-time work after being laid off, Kline insisted on her own terms: chiefly, a four-day workweek. Priceless to her was the freedom to pad around dreamily in her slippers on Friday mornings. Downshifters like Kline cling to the promise of three things: more time, less stress and more balance. It's a fairly uncapitalistic brew, and to my knowledge only one advertiser has ever tried to sell it. In a network TV ad for the Mormon Church some years ago, a little boy walks tentatively into a board-meeting-in-progress, a tableful of men in suits. He shuffles over to the fellow at the end of the table, peers up and says, "Dad, is time really worth money?" The room falls silent. The boy has his father's attention. "Why yes, Jimmy, it is." Whereupon the kid plunks his piggy bank down on the table. "Well, I'd like to play ball after dinner."

Culture jammers are different from all of the downshifters thus far described. They aren't just trying to get themselves off the consumer treadmill and make more time for their kids. They dissent because they have a strong gut feeling that our culture has gone scandalously wrong and they just can't participate in it anymore. The old American dream of endless acquisition sickens them; it enervates them. For jammers downshifting is not simply a way of adjusting our routines; it's adopting a lifestyle of defiance against a culture run amok, a revolutionary step toward a fundamental transformation of the American way of life.

In *Small Is Beautiful*, a key book in the downshifting canon, E. F. Schumacher sets up an exquisitely sensible template for living. The point of life, he says, is "to obtain the maximum of well-being with the minimum of consumption." This idea is so profoundly simple that it may well become the credo—the cool—of the twenty-first century. It applies in all areas of culture, from food to cars to fashion. "It would be the height of folly . . . to go in for complicated tailoring when a much more beautiful effect can be achieved by the skillful draping of uncut material," Schumacher writes. By this reasoning, it's cooler to ride a bike than cruise around in an air-conditioned BMW. Or to wear a plain white T-shirt than, say, a $125 Ashcroft Freddy Couples golf shirt. It's true, of course. And the truly cool have always known it.

Uncooling Fast Food

Buying and eating food has, like any act of consumption, political and even moral implications. "Every decision we make about food is a vote for the kind of world we want to live in," wrote Frances M. Lappé in her classic little book, *Diet for a Small Planet*. Every purchase of a can of Coke or a trucked-in Chilean nectarine initiates a multinational chain of responses that we simply can't afford to ignore.

Even when we exercise some discretion—watch what we eat when we can, pay attention to whether we're buying Maxwell House coffee (a Philip Morris brand) or Nescafé or whole coffee beans from Sumatra— we can still be duped at the supermarket level. That's because we have allowed our eating habits to be shaped by transnational agribusiness. In the heavily concentrated food industry, the likes of Archer Daniels Midland ("supermarket to the world"), Cargill (the world's largest agribusiness) and Philip Morris (one of the world's largest food corporations) are framing our choices.

Food corporations are formidable opponents because so much of what they do is invisible. One of the things they do is cut us off from the source of our food—a concept known as "distancing."

Distancing is a nasty bit of business, but it shouldn't surprise us. As

Brewster Kneen, author of *Invisible Giant,* puts it, we are "distanced" from our mother's breast the moment a baby bottle is inserted into our mouth. "From that moment on, corporate America gets involved, hawking processed 'junior' foods and baby foods that contain lots of salt, sugar and chemicals. Thus we become eager consumers of Kentucky Fried Chicken, Doritos, Pizza Hut and Pepsi (all the same company) later in life." Eventually, we find ourselves participating in the ultimate act of distancing: eating a genetically altered tomato whose mother plant does not even exist.

The average pound of food in America travels 1,300 miles before it reaches a kitchen table. That's inefficient and unsustainable. Demarketing food involves closing the gap between the source and the plate. It means turning away from fast foods and superstores and embracing farmers' markets and the family kitchen; away from hothouse tomatoes and toward your own local supplier, and eventually, perhaps, your own garden plot. These decisions will change your life, if you have the appetite for the journey.

The commitment involves cutting, bit by bit, the food megacorporations out of your life. This is not so different from weaning yourself off a destructive yet magnetic relationship with another human being. Every time you change your mind and don't slip into McDonald's for a quickie, every time you squirt some lemon into a glass of water instead of popping open a Coke, every time you decide to put that jar of Maxwell House coffee back on the shelf, you strike the gong of freedom.

When a groundswell of people train themselves to do all of these things, to demarket on a daily, personal level, we are applying the bottom jaw of the Strategic Pincer. The top jaw of the pincer is a series of radio and TV campaigns that ridicule the fast/junk-food industry. Working from both ends—bottom up and top down—the pincer will transform the way America, and the world, eats.

Junk food is one of the most frequently advertised products on TV; that makes it a big target. Today, food jammers take on the junk-food corporations the way antismoking activists locked horns with the tobacco industry in the '70s. They try to "contaminate" junk food in the public mind. Every time an antijunk-food ad ("Fact: Over 50 percent of the calories in this Big Mac come from fat") airs, a replicating meme is planted. Every time an uncommercial appears on TV attacking those companies, their brands are a little bit uncooled.

Suppose one day a car full of teenage kids drives by the Golden Arches and everyone wants to stop for a bite. But one kid, inspired by a TV subvert he saw the night before, makes a crack about the McDonald's employee standing over the 900-degree french-fry cooker, wearing the funny hat, making minimum wage and saying, "Somebody remind me again why I'm not selling drugs?" His friends chuckle. And maybe they all still stop at McDonald's for that meal. But now they're thinking about McDonald's in a new way. The oppositional meme has been planted.

In the nutrition wars, change is afoot. People are rethinking their food and where it comes from. The idea is catching on that each of us should "have" a personal farmer, the way we now have a doctor, lawyer or dentist, a single individual we can trust to supply us with healthy, safe, flavorful produce. So are farmers' markets where regional producers (and only regional producers) are invited to sell their wares. So are community "box schemes" where hampers of fresh fruit and vegetables—whatever's in season—are delivered direct from local farms to consumers' doors. Out with Wonder Bread from megamarkets, in with community-supported agriculture, say the new food seers. Down with policies that encourage industrial, irradiated, bioengineered food production to the detriment of everybody but agribusiness. Up with flavor! Up with nutrition! Up with local control!

Uncooling Calvin

When fashion and cosmetics advertisers market our very physiognomies as renewable, reinventable commodities, we are dehumanized. We are used up and discarded. In the semiotics of advertising, we are "cut." The young woman made to feel insecure about her sexuality stops behaving authentically. She either comes on like a virago or, conversely, starts staying home Friday nights to compose sad poetry from her black heart. Likewise, a young man made to feel insecure about his sexuality either withdraws or grows angry and aggressive and starts taking what he wants.

As no other company in the last fifteen years, Calvin Klein has commodified sex, and in the process brutalized our notions of sexuality and self-worth. The man at the head is a pioneer. He's credited with creating the ad strategy of moving fashion ads from magazines to outdoor billboards and bus cards, and of trumpeting the era of the commercial nude.

Most people remember his 1995 campaign in which young models were crudely filmed in cheesy wood-paneled basements as an adult voice called instructions from the wings. The ads reeked of chicken-hawk porn. *Advertising Age*'s Bob Garfield called it "the most profoundly disturbing campaign in TV history." The spots so offended public sensibility that they prompted an investigation by the U.S. Justice Department to determine if the models were underage or child-porn laws were violated.

When I saw those ads I felt an animal rage stirring inside me. This was an affront much worse than simple Skinner-box behaviorism. Calvin wasn't just trying to program young people's choice of jeans, he was down in the subbasement of consciousness, where the very rudiments of identity are formed.

I could imagine Mr. Klein rubbing his hands with glee. Here he was exploiting one of our final taboos and milking the controversy he created for all it was worth. From a marketing perspective, he was in a win-win situation and the more controversy the better.

Imagine, for a moment, that the logo cK were the man, Calvin Klein. Would we feel any differently about the way he goes about his business? Calvin Klein is very interested in your teenage daughter. You see him flirting with her. He propositions her. He unzips her pants. He touches her. He sleeps with her. Finally, he prostitutes her. He degrades her sexuality for his profit and then, when she has paid out—literally and figuratively—he dumps her.

OBSESSION FETISH
A 30-SECOND TV SPOT

A collage of cool, sexy, eerily familiar fashion images, complete with hip music and quick jump cuts.

Close-up on model.
Voice: "Why do nine out of ten women feel dissatisfied with some aspect of their own bodies?"

The model vomits into the toilet.

Voice: "The beauty industry is the beast."

MEME WARFARE TONIGHT 1-800-663-1243

If you discovered someone had done this to your daughter, you'd probably call up a couple of your big-armed friends and pay the sonofabitch a visit. Yet what's the difference, in the end, between the cK ads and imagery exploiting her and Calvin doing it himself? Psychically speaking, a hole is still a hole, whether it was made with an auger or a billion drops of water.

The first stage of demarketing our bodies involves realizing the true source of our self-esteem problems. It's important to understand that we ourselves are not to blame. Body-image distortions, eating disorders, dieting and exercise addictions—these are intensely personal issues, fought with therapy and lonely sessions of clandestine vomiting after dinner. They're our responsibility, *but they are not our fault*. The issue is primarily a cultural and a corporate one, and that's the level on which it must be tackled. We must learn to direct our anger, not inwardly at ourselves, but outwardly at the beauty industry.

Can the almighty fashion industry be uncooled? In some ways, its dependence on fads and trends makes it exceptionally vulnerable. Targeting one company—one man—is a good beginning. Cutting significantly into Calvin Klein's sales will effectively launch the crusade to take back our bodies. Uncooling Calvin will send a shock wave through the whole industry; it will rattle the cosmetics companies, which now account for the largest individual product group (with the highest markups) in most big department stores; and it will affect women's magazines, which have generated enormous profits by convincing women they are sexual machines. It will send a powerful message that the pageant is over, and that from now on beauty will no longer be defined by the likes of Mr. Klein—or any other Mister.

The jammer's best strategy is to plant antifashion memes on popular TV shows such as CNN's *Style with Elsa Klensch* and its Canadian knockoff, *Fashion File*. I hear fear in network executives' voices every time I try to buy airtime for our "Obsession Fetish" campaign on the big three networks or CNN. These executives practically do contortions trying to explain why they won't sell us the airtime; they know that Calvin Klein and indeed the whole fashion industry would significantly cut back their TV advertising budgets as soon as our campaign started. The fashion industry is already held in disdain by many. The only thing that keeps its bubble aloft is this uncontested billion-dollar presence in women's magazines and on the airwaves. When we win the legal right to buy airtime and challenge the industry on TV, that bubble will burst. And then it will be Calvin's and the industry's turn to feel insecure.

Uncooling the Car

Jammers are now targeting automobiles as the next pariah industry. We want to sever the intimate connection between people and their cars, just as we cut the intimate connection between people and cigarettes. We want auto executives to feel just as squeezed and beleaguered as tobacco executives. We want them to have a hard time looking their kids in the eye and explaining exactly what they do for a living.

Resistance to private cars is already building. In San Francisco thousands of bicyclists roll out of the Embarcadero district, snarling traffic; a few hold up a giant effigy of Willie Brown, the mayor who labeled cyclists "terrorists." In Portland, Oregon, the city council experiments with an Amsterdam-style system of free commuter bicycles, which can be borrowed and returned at various points downtown. In Canada, jammers air anticar ads, breaking the automobile industry's uncontested, uninterrupted fifty-year run on TV.

Across the First World, pressure mounts for more bike lanes on urban streets. Several high-profile architects and planners weigh in with striking visions of the ecofriendly cities of the next era. Some big oil corporations, British Petroleum among them, finally accept some responsibility for global warming and pledge to sink money into research to develop cleaner petroleum products. Around the world a half dozen companies compete to produce commercially viable fuel cells that will power cars at highway speeds with fewer harmful by-products. Seth Dunn of the WorldWatch Institute likens what's happening now to a full-circle return, one century later, to "engineless carriages."

On a strategic level, however, much work remains to be done.

More than any other product, the car stands as a symbol of the need for a true-cost marketplace, wherein the price you pay for a car reflects *all* the costs of production and operation. That doesn't just mean paying the manufacturing cost plus markup, plus oil, gas and insurance. It means paying for the pollution, for building and maintaining the roads, for the medical costs of accidents and the noise and the aesthetic degradation caused by urban sprawl. It means paying for traffic policing and for military protection of oil fields and supply lines.

The true cost of a car must also include the real but hard-to-estimate environmental cost *to future generations* of dealing with the oil- and ozone-depletion and climate-change problems the car is creating today. If we added up the best available estimates, we'd come to a startling conclusion: The fossil fuel–based automobile industry is being subsidized by unborn generations to the tune of hundreds of billions of dollars every year. Why should they have to pay to clean up our mess?

In the true-cost marketplace of the future, no one will prevent you from driving. You will simply have to pay the real cost of piloting your ton of metal, spewing a ton of carbon out of the tailpipe every year. Your private automobile will cost you, by some estimates, around $100,000. And a tankful of gas, $250.

Moving gradually over a ten-year period toward true-cost driving (giving the global automakers clear signals for long-term planning) would force us to reinvent the way we get around. When the majority of people can no longer afford to drive, enormous public demand for monorails, bullet trains, subways and streetcars would emerge. Automakers would design ecofriendly alternatives: vehicles that recycle their own energy, human- and fuel-powered hybrids, lightweight solar vehicles. Citizens would demand more bike lanes, pedestrian paths and car-free downtowns. And a paradigm shift in urban planning would ensue.

About five or so years into the transition period, personal automobiles would become more trouble than they're worth. People would start enjoying their calmer lifestyles and the new psychogeography of their cities. The rich car owner still cruising through town belching carbon would become the object of scorn and mockery.

In many ways the true-cost marketplace is the ultimate, all-purpose demarketing device. Every purchase becomes a demarketing loop. Every transaction penalizes the "bad" products and rewards the "good." Jammers envision a global, true-cost marketplace in which the price of *every* product tells the ecological truth. The price of a pack of cigarettes would include the extra burden it places on the health care system; the price of an avocado would reflect the real cost of flying it over thousands of miles to your supermarket; the cost of nuclear energy (if indeed we can afford it) would include the estimated cost of storing the radioactive waste in the Earth's crust for up to tens of millions of years.

True cost is a simple but potent way to redesign the global economy's basic incentives in a relatively uncharged political atmosphere. Conservatives like the idea because it's a logical extension of their free-market philosophy. Progressives like it because it involves a radical restructuring of the status quo. Governments like it because it gives them a vital new function to fulfill: that of calculating the true costs of products, levying ecotaxes and managing our bioeconomic affairs for the long term. And environmentalists like it because it may be the only way to achieve sustainability in our lifetimes.

Uncooling the Spectacle

Demarketing and the true-cost economy are the metamemes that bring the culture jammers' revolution together. It all sounds pretty ambitious, but the first steps are straightforward. Using a methodical, systematic social marketing campaign, we start at the personal level and grow in scope. We begin by demarketing our bodies, our minds, our children. Then we join with like-minded jammers to demarket whole systems. We go after our chief social and cultural rituals, now warped beyond recognition by commercial forces, and try to restore their original authenticity. Mother's Day, Easter, Halloween, Thanksgiving, Christ-

Nothing™
What you've been looking for

mas: All are ripe for demarketing. All can be reclaimed.

Students insist on ad-free learning environments. Voters demand that election advertising be replaced with televised town hall–type meetings in which the candidates face the electorate directly. Athletes refuse to endorse unethical companies. Fans insist that stadiums be named after their heroes, not corporations. Reporters make sure that advertorials are not part of their job descriptions. Artists, writers and filmmakers work on product marketing as well as social marketing campaigns. Families get food from their gardens and "therapy" from each other, from friends, neighbors and community.

We reverse the spin cycle. We demarket our news, our entertainments, our lifestyles and desires—and, eventually, maybe even our dreams.

TV RATE CARD

Typical rates for a 30-second timeslot:

Super Bowl (national)	$1,500,000
CBS Evening News (national)	$55,000
MTV (national)	$4,100
CNN Headline News (national)	$3,000
Late evening news (local)	$750
Saturday morning cartoons (local)	$450
Late night movies (local)	$100

Call your local stations for exact rates.

MEDIA CARTA

Freedom has always been Western civilization's most powerful metameme. The idea of a free citizenry was born with the ancient Greek notion of "democracy" and has continued to evolve ever since. The English Magna Carta gave it weight and permanence. When the meme spread to the New World, it inspired the end of slavery; later, it led to universal suffrage and the dream of equality among all people.

The march of freedom has been humankind's gradual awakening. We have come to accept the simple truth that oppression does not have to stand. We live under no one's thumb. In every way we control our own destiny.

At the heart of freedom lies the freedom to talk to one another—to communicate. That, too, is as old as the ancient Greeks, who recognized the right of citizens to express their opinions. When the world's first mass medium—the printing press—was introduced, it became clear that "freedom of opinion" was not enough to guarantee free speech (many "Gutenberg revolutionaries" were censored and repressed when they tried to express their opinions about kings and popes). So the higher notion of freedom of expression was born.

Article XI of the 1789 French Declaration of the Rights of Man and of the Citizen asserts that "the free communication of ideas and opinions is one of the most precious rights of man." Since then the principle of freedom of information has been enshrined in all the universal and regional declarations and conventions relating to human rights.

Article 13 of the 1979 American Convention on Human Rights reads, in part: "*The right of expression may not be restricted by indirect methods or means, such as the abuse of government or private controls over newsprint, radio broadcasting, . . . or any other means tending to impede the communication and circulation of ideas and opinions.*"

On December 10, 1948, freedom of information was enshrined in the Universal Declaration of Human Rights, whose article 19 is the most categorical expression thereof: "*Everyone has the right . . . to freedom of opinion and expression; this right includes freedom . . . to seek, receive and impart information and ideas through any media and regardless of frontiers.*"

Half a century after the signing of the Universal Declaration of Human Rights, citizens have access to a mind-numbing amount of information. Hundreds of newspapers and magazines are at our fingertips. The five-hundred-channel universe has turned out to be a conservative guess. CNN beams news live around the world twenty-four hours a day. Cyberspace expands exponentially from the Big Bang of the digital revolution. It would be easy to conclude, in this climate, that the long struggle for freedom of opinion, expression and speech is finally over.

But it's not.

In the past twenty years, an unprecedented situation has developed with grave implications for democracy and freedom of speech: the emergence of a global communications cartel. The flow of information worldwide is controlled by an ever-shrinking number of transnational media corporations led by a handful of giants—Tele-Communications Inc. (T.C.I.), Time Warner, Disney, Bertelsmann, General Electric, Viacom and Rupert Murdoch's News Corporation. The great power of these organizations lies in their vertical integra-

tion. They can produce a film and distribute it through their own par-
tially or fully owned theater chain, promote it through their own TV
networks, play the soundtrack on their own radio stations and sell the
merchandising spinoffs at their own amusement parks. A property
can enter this vertical chain at any point and be spun in either direction. A film becomes a book, a hit single, then a TV show, a video
game, a ride. Among them, the media giants have the means to produce a never-ending flow of social spectacles, and to nurture them,
feed them, massage them and keep them resonating in the public
mind. With the exception of a few wild domains still left here and
there (public-access TV, pirate radio, zines, some unexplored reaches
of cyberspace), the media megacorps have pretty well colonized the
whole global mindscape and "developed" it into a theme park—a jolly,
terrifyingly homogenized Las Vegas of the mind.

What does freedom of speech mean in this kind of mental environment?

What can you as an individual do if you don't like an ad campaign,
the violence on TV, the way your local TV station covers the news, or
the way a corporation or the government is manipulating the public
agenda? Well . . . you can send a letter to the editor of your local newspaper, call in to a radio talk show or take your complaint to an advertising industry association like the American Association of Advertising
Agencies (AAAA) or the Canadian Advertising Association (CAA). You
can phone a TV station or vent your spleen to the media watchdogs, the
Federal Communications Commission (FCC) and the Canadian Radio-
Telecommunications Commission (CRTC). If you're really angry (and
somewhat organized), you can attend FCC hearings and try to revoke a
TV license. Or you can become a media producer, write your own script
and try to break into the information chain with your own documentary. If you're rich, you can bankroll your own films and documentaries.
If you're very rich, you can buy a TV station. If you're filthy rich, you
can amass a media empire. Each stage of participation takes you higher
on what I call the "ladder of truth." Only a very few people ever get
beyond the bottom rungs.

On the lower rungs, our democracy seems to work quite well. Newspapers print lots of letters to the editor, radio talk shows debate the hot issues of the day, media and advertising watchdogs deal with hundreds of complaints every year. But how do you climb the ladder of truth and get your voice heard in the higher echelons of public discourse?

David Grossman has thought a lot about this. A former U.S. Army officer and the author of the Pulitzer Prize–nominated *On Killing: The Psychological Cost of Learning to Kill in War and Society*, he has made a personal crusade of spreading the word on the incontrovertible link between TV violence and real-world crime. More than two hundred studies have identified a clear cause-and-effect relationship, and every credible agency from the American Medical Association to the Surgeon General's Office to the United Nations has accepted the conclusion. Yet this news has somehow escaped most American parents. If they realized the impact of TV violence on their kids, they would hardly be so cavalier about their kids' viewing habits (or for that matter their own), Grossman suspects.

These people cannot be warned effectively, because the most powerful and far-reaching delivery system for the message won't broadcast it. Even though Grossman has been contacted many times by apparently enthusiastic television producers, no story on him or the TV-crime link has ever aired on network TV (with one exception, when CNBC gave him the hook after twenty seconds). "Every time the story gets to a higher level, it's killed," he says plainly. Grossman happens to live in Jonesboro, Arkansas, where a local student recently went on a schoolyard shooting rampage. As an expert on the psychology of assassination, Grossman was besieged by the media, did many international radio and newspaper interviews, and was contacted by more than a dozen network TV producers. But his TV spots never ran. "Without fail, remorse or hesitation, when the networks found out where I was coming from (that is, ready to implicate TV as a probable culprit in the tragedy), they'd have nothing to do with me," Grossman says. "The magnitude of the stonewalling is staggering."

What to do then? How do you get the message out when you have no access to the messenger? Grossman's long-term strategy involves three points of attack: education, legislation and litigation. Educate by every other means but TV "until there's a groundswell of outrage," until the conspicuous absence of TV coverage of an enormous national story becomes the obvious story in itself. Legislate change by lobbying for major amendments to broadcast regulations, or the wholesale replacement of the FCC. Institute class-action suits for damages against the industry, much like the ones that have been brought against the tobacco industry. "The broadcasters may be powerful enough to buy candidates and influence elections, but they can't buy every jury of twelve people in the U.S. When a jury sees the unassailable evidence, we've won." Grossman imagines a group of people who have already been victimized in a high-profile incident like the one in Jonesboro banding together and launching an action that simply cannot be ignored. "Parents of the shooter and the parents of the victims have to both agree that one of the criminals here is the TV networks. And then we hold the networks' feet to the fire."

Grossman is proof that a committed individual can climb the ladder of truth, but his dilemma points to a disturbing lack of democracy at the heart of our mass media. Nor is TV violence the only subject too taboo for the networks to touch. Think of TV addiction, arguably North America's number one mental health problem. Or unsustainable overconsumption by the affluent people of the First World. When is the last time you saw a network show (or a citizen-produced advocacy ad) on these subjects?

Here's the point: The ideas, expressions and concerns of individual citizens no longer matter very much. Culture isn't created from the bottom up by the people anymore—it's fed to us top-down by corporations. Under current conditions, real debate is impossible. Real democracy is impossible. Real change is impossible.

Media Carta is a media reform movement to take back the cultural power to which all citizens are entitled—to reclaim our airwaves and the rest of our mental environment so that we can start telling our own stories and learn how to talk to each other again.

Occasionally, we get a glimpse of how this new paradigm might work. In December 1996, the worst snowstorm in a century hit the Pacific Northwest. In Victoria, British Columbia, home to Canada's mildest climate (think Seattle with half the rain), five feet of snow fell. A dead calm settled over the paralyzed city. Victoria was about as prepared for this as Troy was for the Greeks. The city had only a couple of snowplows. For days, no cars moved. People were trapped in their houses. Virtually no stores were open because the employees couldn't get to work. The brave ventured out, pulling supplies on sleds. A city of 300,000 was essentially plunged back to pre-Industrial Revolution days.

I mention this because a fascinating media story grew out of that storm. What happened at a local radio station called CFAX emerged as an example of the potential use (and long-forgotten past use) of public airwaves as a democratic medium.

A couple of CFAX employees who had been marooned in the building by the snow decided to open up a kind of jungle telegraph of emergency information. Any citizens who could trudge to the station were put on the air, to tell the city what they had seen out there: someone needed help in saving a greenhouse on the Island Highway. An old couple was stranded and in trouble on Pandora Avenue. A family harboring two dozen refugee motorists in Fernwood was running out of food.

Soon everyone knew that CFAX (and, to a lesser extent, the Internet) was the source of breaking news, delivered by individual sets of eyes and ears. Every newscast contained information valuable to someone. Every broadcast, in the widest possible sense, served the public interest.

It struck many Victorians that this was the way the world was supposed to work. The private voices that came over the Victoria airwaves may not have been broadcasting-school smooth, but they rang with the clarity of the real. They weren't flacking some story that commercial interests wanted to propagate. They had something to tell and nothing to sell. The citizens responded. Isolated individuals suddenly felt part of the larger chain; in the Buddhist sense, everyone became enlightened.

The CFAX case is obviously a unique one—you couldn't repeat it, wouldn't want to repeat it, on a national scale. But it does contain the essence of what we're trying to reclaim here. Victorians never felt more part of a community than they did during that storm, when, for a brief time, the media fulfilled a social agenda and everyone's two cents were welcome and equal. I wonder how many of those people, when the snow had melted and their lives had returned to normal and the commercial pap was back on the air, looked at radio—or media in general—differently. I wonder if any of them thought, This is the way our mass media could be if they had taken a different evolutionary fork in the road.

I told the CFAX tale to a friend of mine who plays devil's advocate to many of my ideas. "So what's your point?" he asked.

"My point is, there needs to be a way to get people talking to each other on radio and TV without commercial mediation."

"There is," he said. "It's called public radio. And public television." He looked into the middle distance. "I can see it now. Kalle's World: all public broadcasting all the time. Commercialism has been weaned from the airwaves. And all these public stations are funded by ever-so-conscientious private listeners and viewers with nothing better to do with their time or money than phone in pledges. Remind me to come over to your place sometime and we'll catch what's on the tube: First we'll watch the puppet show and then we'll watch the half-hour documentary on mulch."

"Congratulations," I replied. "You've managed to completely miss the point. Look, this isn't about enforcing a diet of PBS. It's about opening TV up and letting the commercial memes duke it out with the noncommercial memes until a new balance is reached. I don't want commercialism to be completely purged from broadcasting. But it can't be the one and only voice."

What happens when the commercial voice monopolizes the information delivery systems for years and years? We get used to it. That voice becomes the norm. We cease questioning it. Indeed, we have a hard time even imagining other voices.

When President Clinton made a diplomatic trip to China in June 1998, high-level politicians held a debate to determine whether to allow him to address human-rights issues or to debate President Jiang Zemin live on national TV. Eventually, it was decided that Clinton could have TV access if he agreed, among other things, not to meet later with dissidents in Hong Kong.

Most North Americans find this kind of thing fairly astonishing. That TV access by the world's most powerful leader would need the host government's approval seems ludicrous. That, however, is (as of this writing, at least) the Chinese way. Of course, if China were to scrap its state-controlled media, and citizen-owned media were to be installed in its place, the country would be instantly transformed. Chinese culture would heave.

American broadcasting isn't an Orwellian state-controlled system. It's a commercial, corporate-controlled system, but that control can be, in its own Huxleyan way, just as undemocratic and uncompromising as the Chinese system. If Americans suddenly decided to break up the media monopolies with powerful antitrust legislation; or to reserve a few minutes of every TV broadcast hour for public-generated advocacy messages; or to deploy some other participatory strategy that gives individuals and groups a voice on the public airwaves, American culture would heave, too.

On the surface, the battle for Media Carta—the struggle for who will control the production and distribution of information in the twenty-first century—looks like a very unfair fight. On one side stand the mighty media megacorporations, the government regulators, and a half-century tradition of managing the airwaves as a commercial enterprise. On the other side stands a motley collection of writers, artists, academics, politicized communications professors and high school media-literacy teachers, and a loose global network of NGOs and media and environmental activists. Nevertheless, the underdog has some effective tactical tools at its disposal. On several fronts there are "leverage points," and if we commit to working them simultaneously, they will bring results. Here are some of those leverage points:

- *TV Turnoff Week.* A social ritual every April where citizens reclaim a little time and tranquillity by staying away from the set for one week. The short-term goal is to get enough abstainers on board to depress the Nielsen ratings for that week—a powerful gesture of consumer sovereignty. The broader goal is simply to improve the quality of people's lives.
- *The Two-Minute Media Revolution.* As citizen-produced advocacy uncommercials challenge the status quo on TV, a cyberpetition gathers signatures. The petition demands that the broadcast industry's governing bodies (in the U.S., the FCC; in Canada, the CRTC), when granting broadcast licenses, give two minutes out of every broadcast hour back to the people (advocacy messages would be chosen on a first-come first-served basis from among those who wish to speak). If enough people sign the petition, this strategy will open a hairline crack in the media monopoly.
- *Antitrust Lawsuits.* The U.S. attorney general's 1998 suit against Microsoft is a good example of how potent a tool antitrust legislation can be. If enough fed-up citizens demanded a freer, more diverse cultural environment, the government could be pressured to go after Time Warner, News Corporation and Disney, and limit the number of TV stations, newspapers and radio stations each is allowed to own.
- *The Revocation of Television Licenses.* Thirty years ago, local residents in Boston filed a petition to the FCC to protest the shoddy nightly news broadcasts of their local station. They wanted WHDH-TV to have its license revoked—and they succeeded. WHDH faded to black and a new station under new management was born.

No one since has repeated the Bostonians' success. These days it's almost impossible to unplug trashy TV stations: Licenses only come up for renewal every eight years, the dates aren't advertised and for decades now, whenever a case does come before them, both the FCC and CRTC always come down in favor of the broadcasters.

None of this has deterred Paul Klite, the executive director of the Denver-based Rocky Mountain Media Watch.

Like many others, Klite believes a lot of network programming is unnecessarily, destructively violent, so he put Denver-area newscasts through a sophisticated content analysis he called the "mayhem test." What he found is no surprise: excessive coverage of murders, terrorism, war and disaster. One station's evening news was 47 percent "mayhem." With this data and citizens' petitions in hand, Klite's group lobbied the FCC to deny the renewals of the broadcast licenses of four local stations. Klite argued that Denver TV news is "harming the citizens of Colorado," and that they deserve some protection from such programming.

Klite struck out. In the FCC's view, TV news is protected by the First Amendment, and the networks are free to air whatever news they please.

Despite this setback, Klite's work has pumped new blood into media activism and created an example that other media watchdogs can follow. His work points to a whole new attitude of personal propriety toward the public airwaves, and reminds us that they belong to *us*, not the networks. Most important, he reminds us that we need regulators at the FCC and the CRTC to stop cozying up to broadcasters and start taking some courageous and independent stances in the public interest.

- *Legal Action.* In 1995, Adbusters Media Foundation launched a Canadian Charter legal action against the Canadian Broadcasting Corporation (CBC) for refusing to sell us airtime for our citizen-produced advocacy messages. The case wound its way through the courts until the Supreme Court of Canada threw it out in 1998. The highest court in the land refused to hear it as a constitutional,

PETITION
The Two-Minute Media Revolution

Dear Chairpersons Kennard (FCC) and Bertrand (CRTC),

We the people want access! It is our unwavering conviction that the public interest will best be served if the television licences you grant contain the two-minute media provision. We want broadcasters to set aside two minutes of airtime every hour of every day for citizen-produced messages in exchange for a renewed lease on the public airwaves.

We, the undersigned, put it to you, regulators of our airwaves, to set up a system of direct public access to the most powerful social communications medium of our time, or to let us know why you are unable to do so in a free and democratic society.

name	address	signature

Please sign, photocopy and return this petition to the Media Foundation, 1243 W. 7th Ave. Vancouver, BC, V6H 1B7, Canada. Or fax it to: 604-737-6021. Or find out more and sign the cyberpetition at <www.adbusters.org>

freedom-of-speech issue. The Media Foundation will now take its case to the World Court in The Hague, under Article 19 of the Universal Declaration of Human Rights.

In the U.S., the Media Foundation has been trying since 1993 to launch a First Amendment legal action against NBC, CBS and ABC for routinely refusing to sell us airtime for any of the twenty-odd messages we have tried to air since 1991. We have files full of letters from the networks, plus transcripts of phone conversations with network executives, which prove that not just single thirty-second spots, but *whole classes of information* about transportation, nutrition, fashion and sustainable consumption are systematically being kept off the public airwaves simply because they threaten big-money sponsors.

A First Amendment victory in the U.S. Supreme Court would immediately transform television as we know it today. It would set up a new level playing field between citizens and corporations, and give people and groups a powerful new platform to speak out on the issues that concern them. TV would no longer just transmit commercial propaganda to a passive population but, instead, would become a key site of struggle over the production of meaning. Bit by bit the emptiness of our spectacular culture would be revealed and our currently enforced menu of packaged fun, beauty, heroes and myths would fade. A vibrant new media culture would be born.

Given what's at stake here, you'd think there would be dozens of crusading lawyers eager to sink their teeth into this crucial, high-profile freedom-of-speech case. Unfortunately, that's not so.

Recently, I placed a call to one of America's most powerful litigators, a specialist in First Amendment issues. I explained our position. When citizens cannot walk into their local TV station and buy airtime, then surely their First Amendment rights are being violated. Aren't they?

His reaction was immediate and almost visceral. He was a fierce defender of the First Amendment, true, but chiefly with respect to how it applies to broadcasters. He seemed to hold their right to free choice above all others.

"In America, I don't think you can compel a publisher or broadcaster to carry a particular message," he said.

"But if a network decides that Nike or McDonald's can buy thirty seconds of airtime and say, 'Buy hamburgers' or 'Buy shoes,' why don't I have the right to buy airtime for my side of the story?"

"You do have your rights, but you can't diminish their rights in order to enforce yours."

I told him I thought my right to speak out on TV was fairly basic, given that these are public airwaves that legally belong to everyone.

"I think that's a fiction," he said. "The air may belong to you, but not the studios and broadcasting facilities of ABC."

I placed a call to another lawyer, this time a high-profile Los Angeles media attorney and former president of the Beverly Hills Bar Association, who turned out to be equally circumspect.

"Networks have the right to quality control," he said. "They have a right to say, 'We won't carry a message that would be offensive to the other sponsors, because we don't want to lose those sponsors.'"

That's the way it all boils down: The broadcaster's right to run a commercial business stands in direct opposition to my right to freedom of speech. I was looking for an advocate who believed that my cause—the cause of the people—had at least equal merit. The Beverly Hills attorney gave me the number of another lawyer to try, and he cordially hung up. The hunt for the First Amendment grail continues.

Only the vigilant can maintain their liberties, and only those who are constantly and intelligently on the spot can hope to govern themselves effectively by democratic procedures. A society, most of whose members spend a great deal of their time not on the spot, not here and now in the calculable future, but somewhere else, in the irrelevant other worlds of sport and soap

opera, of mythology and metaphysical fantasy, will find it hard
to resist the encroachments of those who would manipulate
and control it.

Aldous Huxley was on the mark in the foreword of his revised 1946 edition of *Brave New World*, which perhaps more than any other work of twentieth-century fiction predicted the psychological climate of our wired age. One can draw an easy parallel between "soma"—the pleasure drug issued to citizens of *Brave New World*—and the mass media as we know them today. Both keep the masses tranquilized and pacified, and maintain the social order. Both chase out reason in favor of entertainments and disjointed thought. Both encourage uniformity of behavior. Both devalue the past in favor of sensory pleasures now.

Unlike the people in Orwell's *1984*, who resent being controlled by Big Brother but feel powerless to resist, residents of Huxley's realm willingly participate in their manipulation. They happily take soma. They're in the loop, and, by God, they love it. The pursuit of happiness becomes its own end—there's endless consumption, free sex and perfect mood management. The people are enraptured. They believe they live in Utopia. Only you, the reader (and a couple of "imperfect" characters in the book who somehow ended up with real personalities) know it's Dystopia. It's a hell that can only be recognized by those outside the system.

Our own dystopia, too, can only be detected from the outside—by "outsiders" who for some strange reason did not watch too much TV when they were young; who read a few good books, met a few good people, spent some time living in other cultures, and by some lucky twist of fate were not seduced by The Dream and recruited into the consumer cult of the insatiables.

Although most of us are still stuck in the cult, our taste for soma is souring. Through the haze of manufactured happiness, we are realizing that *we must stop the show*, that our only escape is to halt the flow of soma, to break the communication cartel's monopoly on the production of meaning.

Media Carta is the great human-rights battle of our information age—a great personal, intellectual, social, cultural and legal test. The infrastructure for this battle is already in place. Culture jammers around the world are preparing for the showdown. In the early years of the new millennium, we will spearhead a media reform movement to enshrine the right to communicate as a fundamental human right in the constitutions of all free nations and in the Universal Declaration of Human Rights.

We will save the most precious of all our natural resources: the peace and clarity of our own minds.

System Error-Type 1945 (progress)

REDEFINING PROGRESS

Fifteen hundred eminent scientists, including the majority of all living Nobel Prizewinners, signed a Warning to Humanity in 1992, and fifty-eight world academies of science released a similar document in 1994, warning that the human experiment on Planet Earth is veering out of control. Population growth, overconsumption, inappropriate technological applications and relentless economic expansion are destroying the life-support systems on which our future depends.

Meanwhile, strangely, our politicians, economists and business leaders are wearing banana grins. "We're growing," they beam. "We're putting up more factories, selling more goods, creating more wealth than ever before in the history of mankind."

Never-ending material growth is the cornerstone of our current economic system. There's no such thing as a zero-growth model within its framework. In fact, nothing much but material growth really matters, economists have decreed.

And yet, constant growth within finite terrain is the ideology of the cancer cell. It's madness. It's a madness propagated twenty-four hours a day by the corporate-controlled mass media, which are structurally incapable of offering us the root-cause analyses of our current predicament.

So we're stuck trying to reconcile powerful mixed messages. For most of us the economy remains a mysterious abstract system. As with our microwave oven, we don't know how it works and we don't really want to know. We just keep pushing buttons and hot dinners keep coming out. We think of markets having their own laws that we break at our peril. And we think that economists are learned scientists who, with their arcane but irrefutable logic, are somehow managing the whole affair.

The truth is that we have handed our ecological and economic well-being over to an elite group of professional policymakers who have, at best, only a vague idea of what they are doing. Their "scientifically" managed cycles of "growth" and consumption are wiping out the natural world, though if you put it to them that way, they would deny it. Their idea of "progress" is to sell off the planet's irreplaceable natural capital and call it income—though they would deny that too.

Is there a way out of this social trap—this crisis of meaning? The economics profession won't admit its models are flawed. First World consumers remain blissfully unaware of the havoc wrought by their lifestyles. The commercial broadcast media won't sell airtime for citizen-produced wake-up calls. Governments refuse to acknowledge the astronomical ecological debt we have already accrued to future generations. Most everyone is in denial. Deep down, we all "know" the planet is dying, but nobody wants to talk about it.

Of course there are ways to get the conversation going—strategies for jamming the global economy back onto a sustainable path.

First, we kill all the economists (figuratively speaking). We prove that despite the almost religious deference society extends to them, they aren't untouchable. We challenge their authority, question their credentials. We launch a global media campaign to discredit them. We show how their economic models are fundamentally flawed. We reveal their "science" as a dangerous pseudoscience. We ridicule them on TV. We enlist our own, equally decorated ecological economists to debate them point for point. We pop up in unexpected places like on the local business news, on commercial breaks during the midnight movie and randomly on national prime time.

At the same time, we lay a trap for the G-7 leaders. Our campaign paints them as Lear-like figures, deluded kings unaware of the damage their deepening madness is doing. We demand to know why the issue of overconsumption in the First World is not even on their agenda. In the weeks leading up to their yearly summit meeting, we buy radio and TV spots on stations around the world that dare our leaders to answer the Big Question: "Is Economic 'Progress' Killing the Planet?"

We make those six words blaze in the public imagination. We get ordinary citizens to think about them, policymakers to debate them and students to confront their teachers with them. Little by little we maneuver the leaders into a position where suddenly, at a worldwide press conference, they are forced to respond to a question like this: "Mr. President, how do you measure economic progress? How do you tell if the economy is healthy or sick?"

The President will probably skate. He'll formulate some pat answer about how America has a pretty good report card, what with one of the best GDP growth rates and the record-setting bull run on Wall Street. He'll try to move on. But a few reporters will keep pressing him and the other leaders. They will demand a better answer—a real answer: Should we consider the *Exxon Valdez* spill a "success," since it boosted GDP? What other measures of economic progress besides the GDP are being used? How are losses of natural capital like the disappearing salmon fisheries of the Pacific Northwest being factored into the national accounts? Are the costs of climate change being considered? What about ozone depletion? Desertification? Biodiversity loss?

A point will be reached, either right there at the G-7 press conference or at some future press conference, when it dawns on the world that these seven men and their economic policymakers can't be trusted with the farm. They don't know the answer to the simplest and most fundamental of all questions about the economic system they manage: Are we moving forward or backward?

This escalating war of nerves with the heads of state is the top jaw of our Strategic Pincer. The bottom jaw of the pincer is the work that goes on at a grassroots level, where neoclassical dogma is still being propagated every day. Within university economics departments worldwide, a wholesale mindshift is about to take place. The tenured professors who run those departments, the keepers of the neoclassical flame, are as proud and stubborn as high-alpine goats, and they don't take well to being challenged. But challenge them we will, fiercely, and with the conviction that we are right and they are wrong.

Thomas Kuhn, in his now famous 1962 book *The Structure of Scientific Revolutions*, describes how paradigm shifts in science are very much like political revolutions. They are messy affairs that don't unfold quickly or easily or without the painful overthrow of the people in power.

Kuhn's most profound insight is that, in the real world, contrary to the way scientific progress is supposed to happen, an old paradigm cannot be replaced by new evidence, facts or "the truth." It can only be replaced by another paradigm. In other words, the profession of economics will not change just because its forecasts are wrong, its policies no longer work or its theories are proved unscientific. It will change only when a new maverick generation of economists grabs the old-school practitioners by the scruffs of their necks and throws them out of power.

How to Break the Neoclassical Trance

Start a culture-jamming group on your campus. Try to get postgraduate economics students and at least one professor to join. Then wage meme warfare. Gather potent quotes by famous economic visionaries as rhetorical ammunition.

> *Departments of economics are graduating a generation of idiot savants, brilliant at esoteric mathematics yet innocent of actual economic life.*
>
> —Wassily Leontief, Nobel Prize–winning economist

The standard texts are powerful instruments of disorientation;
for confusing the mind and preparing it for the acceptance of
myths of growing complexity and unreality.
    —Guy Routh, *The Origin of Economic Ideas*

Before economics can progress it must abandon its suicidal for-
malism.
    —Robert Heilbroner

Ridicule neoclassical logic every chance you get. Interrupt lectures.
Argue with your professors after class. Look them in the eye and ask the
same questions you might ask one of the G-7 leaders if you got the
chance: How do you measure economic progress? How do you tell if the
economy is progressing or regressing? If they cannot adequately answer
that question, then question the grounds on which their profession
gives policy advice to governments.

Plan a Real Economics Teach-In on your campus to coincide with
the next G-7 economic summit. Invite an ecological-economics
maverick like Herman Daly, Robert Costanza or Paul Hawken to speak.
Find out what other universities around the world are doing. Get your
hands on the sixty-second "G7-Ecocide" radio and TV spots from
Adbusters Media Foundation. Raise funds.

Air the "G7-Ecocide" message on campus radio in the weeks leading up to the summit. Try to buy a few sixty-second TV spots on your
local evening news on the day the G-7 leaders meet. Issue news releases
announcing your campaign. If a TV station refuses to sell you airtime,
publicize that fact. Fax local newspapers. Phone the TV newsrooms. On
the day the leaders meet, get reporters and TV crews out to cover your
teach-in.

A particularly effective economics teach-in was held at the University of Victoria, British Columbia, in May 1996. Stark white posters,
each with a quote challenging the legitimacy of neoclassical economics'
underlying assumptions, lined the walls to greet students and professors
alike one Monday morning.

G-7 ECOCIDE
60-SECOND TV SPOT

Is the Global Economy

a

Doomsday Machine?

www.adbusters.org

MEME WARFARE TONIGHT 1-800-663-1243

Some students were not amused. "It feels like someone's telling you, 'You're stupid, you're stupid' with every sign," one complained. But the Alternative Economics Committee was prepared to bruise a few egos. Deciding to deconstruct their professors' lesson plans for one day, this group of committed students confronted what they termed "fatal abstractions in economics"—the flaws of the neoclassical paradigm taught as gospel in nearly all North American schools.

Teach-ins work. In the 1960s, student radicals created a forum to address a burning question that was being glossed over or entirely ignored during their classes: Just what was the U.S. doing in Vietnam? The teach-ins that followed involved the brightest minds and the bravest professors and served to both legitimize dissident thought and inspire action.

At UVic, rather than focusing on a single political issue, the students took on the whole paradigm, examining the real-life consequences of neoclassical economics.

The teach-in was a series of hourlong panels that ran all day. Organizers figured they'd have trouble finding faculty willing to challenge the department, but they didn't. Disillusioned academics were burning to air their grievances. Almost all speakers had more to say than their fifteen minutes allowed. The rancor spilled over into a question period.

The economics department sent a lone defender, a professor named Peter Kennedy, who gamely tried to keep up the side. At one point he refuted an opponent's statement by referring the audience to a certain page on a certain syllabus, as if to chastise the speaker for errant study habits. But Professor Kennedy was condescending and could not explain his position in plain language, which spoke volumes about the fundamental problems in the department.

From speaker after speaker, memes flew.

"There's no social security in a world that consumes the biosphere in which we live."

"Nuclear energy is touted as a 'cheap fuel.' But is the waste disposal of spent nuclear fuel factored into the cost?"

Later, Professor Kennedy stepped to the podium for a second time. He stood in front of the crowd, dressed in a casual shirt and jeans. The anger and condescension were gone. "Economists are like weather forecasters," he said. "They explain, but they do not influence, events." He admitted the need for interdisciplinary studies to cross-pollinate and bring studies like economics into the real world. His defense of the holy canon seemed labored. The students had him on the run.

Little insurrections like the one at UVic are seen more and more frequently these days. In 1997, a group of students at Harvard University rebelled against the neoclassical doctrine taught them by Martin Feldstein, a former adviser to President Ronald Reagan. The students held weekly meetings, invited guest speakers and handed out dissenting leaflets at Feldstein's lectures.

So far the rumblings of student discontent have not turned to open defiance. The old-school practitioners like Feldstein live on, reinforced by the politics of tenure, of who gets published and promoted, whose research gets funded, and who gets plucked out of academia for a plum political appointment when the next administration comes to power. Within a global economy that more and more people are realizing is unsustainable and doomed to fail, they toe the party line.

But not for too much longer.

At critical times throughout history, university students have sparked massive protests, called their leaders on their lies and steered their nations in brave new directions. It happened on campuses around the world in the 1960s, and more recently in South Korea, China and Indonesia. Now we have reached another critical historical moment.

It's hard to predict when the protests will begin en masse, or what will trigger them. It could be a crash on Wall Street tomorrow, or climate change suddenly lurching out of control, or some freak happening such as a charismatic economics student from the University of Chicago confronting Alan Greenspan (or the president of the United States) at a news conference in a dramatic showdown—a clash of economic paradigms—that reverberates around the world.

Then, in the months that follow, on campus after campus, the students will chase the old goats out of power and begin the work of reprogramming the doomsday machine.

Vivez sans temps mort!

(Live without dead time).

EPILOGUE: THE MILLENNIAL MOMENT OF TRUTH

In all revolutions, the agents of change—usually a small core of fired-up individuals—reach a personal point of reckoning where to do nothing becomes harder than to step forward. Then come the televised actions, the rebellions on campus, the random acts of defiance in high schools, supermarkets, malls, workplaces. A mass of support accrues. The little daily confrontations escalate. Momentum builds.

And finally the revolution ignites. Very often the ignition spark is a symbolic act that takes the old power structure by surprise, a gesture that becomes a metaphor, living forever. Rosa Parks refuses to give up her seat on the bus. A Vietnam protester feeds a daisy into the barrel of a rifle. A dissident stares down a line of tanks in Tiananmen Square. Nelson Mandela walks out of his prison cell in South Africa. The TV networks refuse to sell airtime for a citizen's ad. These memes penetrate skulls like bullets.

The biggest impediment to revolution is a personal one: our own deep-seated feelings of cynicism and impotence. How can anything we do possibly make a difference? We have trouble accepting radical change as a viable option. Entrenched in a familiar system, we cannot imagine others. It's hard to see our current condition as simply one stage of a never-ending cycle that sooner or later will fall out of vogue and be succeeded—but this is exactly how the world works. Just as psychoanalysis (which Freud compared to the Copernican and Darwinian revolutions, and which was once widely considered the key to understanding human behavior) has pretty much given way to psychopharmacology, and Christianity has been squeezed out in the West by a fluid, New Age-y conception of spirituality, American-style consumer capitalism will also lose favor. One day soon people will get sick of fast food, fancy cars, fashion statements and shopping malls. They will stop buying heavily advertised products because advertising is coercive, tawdry and just increases the cost of the product. They will realize that "the most advanced urban transportation system is not the automobile but . . . *the bicycle,* that the most promising power supplier of the future is not a bigger electric utility grid, but a new kind of . . . *shingle on your roof,* that the most efficient form of residential air conditioning is actually . . . *a good shade tree.*" They will tire of the egocentric life of ungoverned consumption and the media hype that fuels it. When a stretch limo glides by in 2003, the pedestrian reflex won't be to peer through the smoked panes for the celebrity inside, but to curse and mock this ridiculous symbol of decadence and environmental harm. The cool people of the next century will opt out of the spectacle and live spontaneous "lives of playful opportunity." And our children, and their children, will gaze back aghast upon our own time, a period of waste and abandon on a scale so vast it knocked the planet out of whack for a thousand years.

We don't need a million activists to jump-start this revolution. We just need an influential minority that smells the blood, seizes the moment and pulls off a set of well-coordinated social marketing strategies. We need a certain level of collective disillusionment (a point I think we have now reached) and then we need the leaders of the affluent, "First" nations of the world to fumble a world crisis like a stock market collapse or mismanage an environmental crisis like global warming. By waiting

for the right moment and then jamming in unison, I think a global network of a few hundred activists can pull off the coup. Like J. K. Galbraith's archetypal "revolutionary," we will kick in the rotten door and
charge into the vacuum. We create a sudden, unexpected moment of
truth—a global mindshift—from which the corporate/consumerist
forces never fully recover.

In May 1968, the Situationist-inspired Paris riots set off "a chain
reaction of refusal" against consumer capitalism. First students, then
workers, then professors, nurses, doctors, bus drivers and a piecemeal
league of artists, anarchists and *Enragés* took to the streets, erected barri-
cades, fought with police, occupied offices, factories, dockyards, railway
depots, theaters and university campuses, sang songs, issued manifestos,
sprayed slogans like "Live Without Dead Time" and "Down with the
Spectacular-Commodity Culture" all over Paris, and challenged the
established order of their time in the most visceral way. The breadth of
the dissent was remarkable. "Art students demanded the realisation of art;
music students called for 'wild and ephemeral music'; footballers kicked
out managers with the slogan 'football to the football players'; gravedig-
gers occupied cemeteries; doctors, nurses, and the interns at a psychiatric
hospital organised in solidarity with the inmates." For a few weeks, millions of people who had worked their whole lives in offices and factories
broke from their daily routines and . . . *lived.*

It was "the largest general strike that ever stopped the economy of
an advanced industrial country, and the first *wildcat general strike* in
history," and it spread rapidly, first around Paris and France and then
around the world. At the height of the uprising in Paris's Latin Quarter,
fifty thousand people marched in Bonn, and three thousand took to the
streets in Rome. Three days later, students revolted at the University of
Milan. The next day, students staged a sit-in at the University of Miami.
Then skirmishes erupted in Madrid, Berkeley, New York City, Frankfurt
and Santiago. The wave reached London, Vancouver, Dakar, Munich,
Vienna and Buenos Aires, then Tokyo, Osaka, Zurich, Rio, Bangkok,
Düsseldorf, Mexico City, Saigon, La Paz, Chicago, Venice, Montreal and
Auckland. For a few heady weeks a tantalizing question hung in the air:

What if the whole world turned into the Latin Quarter? Could this be the beginning of the first global revolution?

As it turned out, this brief, hot happening the Situationists had helped catalyze stopped short of becoming a full-fledged global mind-shift. The protests petered out, governments restored control and the status quo crept back in. The Situationists failed to get the ball over the line, so to speak, because they were in several respects ahead of their time. The spectacular, mediated world they so compellingly described, and its menacing implications, were too new and strange for people in the '60s to grasp fully. And the Situationists themselves were, I think, caught wrong-footed. They and the students, workers, artists and intellectuals they inspired didn't have their memes figured out. At the height of the uprisings, when they had the ear of the world, they did not know what to say beyond a few cryptic pronouncements. "The Beginning of an Epoch," said the Situationists. "The death rattle of the historical irrelevants," said Zbigniew Brzezinski, the national security adviser to the president of the United States.

The moral for culture jammers is, of course, *Learn from this.* Have a well-thought-out and tested action plan, build a united global front and be ready to scramble to the windward side when the boom swings overhead, as it inevitably will.

We've had thirty years to think about what the Situationists were talking about, and it's finally starting to make sense. In that interval of time, modern media culture has metastasized. Consumer capitalism has triumphed. We're *in* the spectacle. The spectacle is *in* us. We are living in what Guy Debord, in the last years of his life, described as the "integrated spectacle," characterized by "incessant technological renewal; integration of state and economy; generalized secrecy; unanswerable lies; an eternal present."

Today, a confused and deeply troubled population is ready to act out. "Direct our cynicism, direct our rage," they seem to be saying. Thirty years ago, the Situationists had a half-baked idea about *détourning* consumer capitalism, putting power in the hands of the people and constructing a spontaneous new way of life. Now it's up to culture jammers to finish the job.

Two generations of chronic overconsumption, decadence and denial have weakened America™. American cool is now every bit as vulnerable as the Soviet Utopia was ten years ago. A revolution couldn't happen there, but it did. It can't happen here, but it will. This is a momentous occasion and we shouldn't doubt or fear, but celebrate. In the dawn of this new millennium, one dream is ending and another being born.

And I can't think of anything much cooler than that.

Notes

Introduction: Culture Jamming

xi   "Culture Jamming" For more information see the *Culture Jammers Campaign Headquarters*: <www.adbusters.org> and *Adbusters* magazine, 1243 West 7th Avenue, Vancouver, B.C. V6H 1B7, Canada; subscriptions@ adbusters.org: 1-800-663-1243 (in North America only).

xi   On the genesis of "culture jamming": I first came across the term in a 1991 *New York Times* article by cultural critic Mark Dery. It was coined by the San Francisco audio collage band Negativland on their 1994 release entitled *Jamcon '84*, as a tribute to ham radio "jammers," who clog the airwaves with scatological Mickey Mouse impersonations and other pop culture "noise." Early culture jammers put graffiti on walls, liberated billboards, operated pirate radio stations, rearranged products on supermarket shelves, hacked their way into corporate and government computers and pulled off daring media pranks, hoaxes and provocations. A new generation of "jammers" is organizing "critical massing" rallies and "reclaim the streets" parties, launching social marketing TV campaigns, coordinating global events like Buy Nothing Day and TV Turnoff Week, jamming G-7 economic summits, initiating legal actions to revoke the charters of dysfunctional corporations, and pioneering an ever more potent array of cultural interventions.

xiii   "something to sell as well as to tell." This often repeated phrase was coined by George Gerbner, founder of the Cultural Environmental Movement and currently Bell Atlantic Professor of Telecommunication at Temple University, Philadelphia.

xvi   "Revolution is not showing life to people, but making them live." Guy Debord, quoted by Len Bracken, *Guy Debord Revolutionary* (Feral House, 1997), page 110. I first saw this quote on the cover of Bracken's book.

xvi   "We will jam its image factory until it comes to a sudden, shuddering halt." For this phrase, I am indebted to Mark Dery, author of *Culture Jamming: Hacking, Slashing, and Sniping in the Empire of Signs* (Westfield, N.J.: Open Magazine Pamphlet Series, 1993).

xix Marshall McLuhan's "World War III" quote from *Culture Is Our Business* (Ballantine Books, 1970), page 66.

Autumn

4 Elisabeth Kübler-Ross, *On Death and Dying* (Macmillan, 1969).

4 "For two million years our personalities and cultures were shaped by nature." This idea was taken from the preface of Robert Kubey and Mihaly Csikszentmihalyi's *Television and the Quality of Life* (L. Erlbaum, 1990), in which the authors write: "By current estimates the first human beings emerged on Earth approximately 2 million years ago. In this vast stretch of time, approximately 100,000 human generations have lived and died, and yet ours are among the first to live in a world where much of daily experience is shaped by widely shared, instantaneous mass communication."

4 "about as voluptuous a place as you can find on earth . . . " Anne Lamott, *Bird by Bird* (Anchor, 1995).

6 "Psychology As If the Whole Earth Mattered" conference, held at Harvard University, fall 1990. From a report in the *Center Review,* Center for Psychology and Social Change, an affiliate of Harvard.

6 On "our rampant, oblivious consumption . . . is, simply, a sickness," see *Ecopsychology: Restoring the Earth, Healing the Mind*, edited by Theodore Roszak, Mary E. Gomes and Allen D. Kanner (Sierra Club Books, 1995).

9 "Is Everybody Crazy?" Jim Windolf, *The New York Observer*, October 20, 1997.

10 "Worldwide rates of major depression in every age group have risen steadily since the 1940s." Elliot S. Gershon and Ronald O. Rieder, *Scientific American*, September 1992, page 91.

10 "Rates of suicide, unipolar disorder, bipolar disorder and alcoholism have all climbed significantly." Roger Bland, chair of psychiatry at the University of Alberta, in the *Canadian Journal of Psychiatry*, May 1997, as reported by Robin Lawrence in *The Georgia Straight,* June 11, 1998.

10 "The U.S. has a higher rate of depression than almost every other country, and cross-cultural data show that as Asian countries Americanize, their rates of depression increase accordingly." Michael Yapko, *Psychology Today*, May/June 1997.

10   Saul Bellow, *Humboldt's Gift* (Avon, 1975).

12   "We know there's a correlation between TV viewing and voter apathy . . . "
      Michael Morgan and James Shanahan, "Television Viewing and Voting
      1975–1989," *Electoral Studies* (1992), 11(1):3–20.

12   "We know that TV viewing is linked to childhood obesity . . . " Ross E.
      Andersen, "TV Viewing Linked to Childhood Obesity," *Journal of the
      American Medical Association* (1998), 279:938–942.

15   Jerry Mander, *Four Arguments for the Elimination of Television* (Quill,
      1978).

15   "Regular TV programming averaged ten technical events per minute and
      commercials twenty. Twenty years later these figures have doubled. MTV
      delivers sixty events per minute . . . " John de Graaf, *The Balaton Bulletin,*
      Fall 1997, page 24.

17   "The average North American witnesses five acts of violence . . . per hour
      of prime-time network TV . . . " This statistic was provided by George
      Gerbner, Bell Atlantic Professor of Telecommunication, Temple Univer-
      sity, Philadelphia.

17   "Two recent studies turned up conflicting results, and the head of one
      research team . . . " Michael Sunnan, research director of the Center for
      Communications Policy at UCLA, quoted in *The Globe and Mail Canada,*
      April 28, 1998.

19   "Every day, an estimated 12 billion display ads, 3 million radio commer-
      cials, and more than 200,000 TV commercials are dumped into North
      America's collective unconscious." From a rough calculation by Rick
      Crawford, postgraduate researcher, Department of Computer Science,
      University of California, Davis.

19   "Three thousand marketing messages per day." Mark Landler, Walecia Kon-
      rad, Zachary Schiller and Lois Therrien, "What Happened to Advertising?"
      Business Week, September 23, 1991, page 66. Leslie Savan in *The Sponsored
      Life* (Temple University Press, 1994), page 1, estimated that "16,000 ads
      flicker across an individual's consciousness daily." I did an informal survey
      in March 1995 and found the number to be closer to 1,500 (this included
      all marketing messages, corporate images, logos, ads, brand names, on TV,
      radio, billboards, buildings, signs, clothing, appliances, in cyberspace, etc.,
      over a typical twenty-four-hour period in my life).

19 "I think of those brainwashing experiments conducted by Dr. Ewen Cameron . . ." Bruce Grierson, "Soul Shock," *Adbusters*, Winter 1998, page 18.

21 "anti-language," a coinage of social critic George Steiner, was invoked in this context by Jonathon Dee in "But Is It Advertising?" *Harper's*, January 1999, page 66.

21 "Adbusters Media Foundation" is a Vancouver, B.C.–based nonprofit society that publishes *Adbusters* magazine, runs the *Culture Jammers Campaign Headquarters* on the World Wide Web and creates social marketing campaigns through its PowerShift advocacy advertising agency. Adbusters Media Foundation, 1243 West 7th Avenue, Vancouver, B.C. V6H 1B7, Canada; <www.adbusters.org>; adbusters@adbusters.org.

24 "Most information has long since stopped being useful for us . . . " Neil Postman, *Technopoly* (First Vintage Books, 1993).

25 "A 1998 survey of eleven- to fifteen-year-old boys and girls . . . " Kunda Dixit, *Media Asia*, Summer 1998, page 95.

25 "In a dozen Asia-Pacific countries surveyed by the A. C. Nielsen company . . ." Normandy Madden, *Advertising Age International*, July 13, 1998.

26 "Everytown, U.S.A.": Rachel Carson, *Silent Spring* (Houghton Mifflin, 1962).

33 "Soviet dissidents used to talk about a 'public sphere of discourse' . . . " Taken from Jonathon Rowe, "The Tyranny of the Airwaves," *Adbusters*, Winter 1991, page 10.

34 "Ninety percent of news editors surveyed in a 1992 Marquette University study . . . " Lawrence C. Soley and Robert L. Craig, "Advertising Pressures on Newspapers: A Survey," *Journal of Advertising*, Volume XXI, Number 4, December 1992.

34 "The PBS flagship *NewsHour*, which is underwritten by Archer Daniels Midland . . . " "Stories TV Doesn't Tell," *The Nation*, June 8, 1998, page 7.

34 "Double-click on 'Rocky Mountain High' and you'll find yourself at the virtual headquarters of the record company selling a boxed set of Denver's greatest hits." Taken from Ronald K. L. Collins, *Adbusters*, Winter 1998, page 59.

35 "In 1997, Chrysler, one of the five largest advertisers in the U.S., sent letters to one hundred newspaper and magazine editors . . . " Gail Johnson, *Adbusters*, Spring 1998, page 19. Confirmed by Alan Miller, Communications Department, at Chrysler's Auburn Hills, Michigan, office.

37 The laugh-track scenario was inspired by an article titled "Oka the Promised Land," submitted to *Adbusters* by Kathleen Moore, May 1995.

39 "Reebok paid Tristar pictures a million and a half bucks . . . " "Sneaky Business," *Entertainment Weekly*, January 24, 1997.

40 Richard Condon, *The Manchurian Candidate* (F. A. Thorpe, 1959).

44 Sherry Turkle, *Life on the Screen: Identity in the Age of the Internet* (Simon & Schuster, 1995).

44 Ann Beattie, "The Occidental Tourist," *Esquire*, September 1988, page 198.

45 Edmund Carpenter, *Oh, What a Blow That Phantom Gave Me!* (Holt, Rinehart and Winston, 1973), page 3.

46 Fay Weldon, *Wicked Women* (Atlantic Monthly Press, 1997).

46 "the first concentrated study of the social and psychological effects of the Internet, a two-year effort by Carnegie Mellon University . . . " *The New York Times*, August 30, 1998.

46 John Irving, *A Prayer for Owen Meany* (Morrow, 1989).

Winter

51 "The Cult You're In" chapter is based on Kono Matsu, "The Cult You're In," *Adbusters*, Summer 1998, pages 32–33.

56 The first International TV Turnoff Week was launched by Adbusters Media Foundation in 1994. See *Adbusters*, Summer 1994, page 24. TV Free America launched U.S. TV Turnoff Week in 1995.

62 The first International Buy Nothing Day was held on September 24, 1992, the brainchild of Vancouver, B.C., artist Ted Dave. It has since grown into a worldwide celebration of simple living. Now held on the last Friday of every November (in some countries on the last Saturday), it is called *Kauf Nix Tag* in Austria, *Niet-Winkeldag* in Belgium, *Älä Osta Mitään Päivä* in

Finland, *La Journée sans Achats* in France, *Kauf Nix Tag* in Germany, *Niet-Winkeldag* in the Netherlands, *Nullkoptagen* in Norway, *Dzien bez zakupow* in Poland, *Dan brez nakupov* in Slovenia, *No Shop Day* in the U.K., *Kopva-grardagen* in Sweden and *Nanimo Kawanai Hi* in Japan.

63   "a bureaucratic society of controlled consumption." Henri Lefebvre, *Critique of Everyday Life* (English translation, Verso, 1991), as quoted in *Baudrillard for Beginners*, Chris Horrocks and Zoran Jevtic (Icon Books Ltd., 1996), page 8.

65   "The Unofficial History of America™" Much of the inspiration for this chapter came from a little booklet called *Taking Care of Business—Citizenship and the Charter of Incorporation*, by Richard L. Grossman and Frank T. Adams (1993, Charter, Ink., P.O. Box 806, Cambridge, MA 02140). Also useful for an early history of corporations in the U.S. is David C. Korten, *When Corporations Rule the World* (Berrett-Koehler Publishers, 1995).

67   "Limits were placed on how big and powerful companies could become." Grossman and Adams, page 8.

67   "The two hundred or so corporations that were operating . . . by the year 1800 were each kept on a fairly short leash." Grossman and Adams, page 7.

67   "In 1832, President Andrew Jackson vetoed a motion. . . " Grossman and Adams, page 12.

68   "President Abraham Lincoln . . . warned . . . , 'corporations have been enthroned . . . ' " David R. Loy, *A Buddhist Critique of Transnational Corporations* (professor, Faculty of International Studies, Bunkyo University, Chigasaki, Japan. <www.igc.apc.org/bpf/think.html>).

68   "In *Santa Clara County* v. *Southern Pacific Railroad* . . . " Grossman and Adams, page 20.

68   "Justice William O. Douglas concluded of *Santa Clara* . . . " Grossman and Adams, page 20.

69   "The shift amounted to a kind of coup d'état . . . " Loy, *A Buddhist Critique of Transnational Corporations.*

69   "fifty-one of the world's hundred largest economies were corporations, not countries." "Was Democracy Just a Moment?" *The Atlantic Monthly*, December 1997, page 71.

70   "a student named Jennifer Beatty stages a protest against corporate sponsorship . . ." Kari Lydersen, *Chicago Ink*, April 1998. Also *Adbusters*, Summer 1998, page 56.

70   "a student named Mike Cameron wears a Pepsi T-shirt on . . . 'Coke
Day' . . ." Frank Swoboda, *The Washington Post*, March 26, 1998. Also
Adbusters, Summer 1998, page 56.

70   "moms and dads push shopping carts down the aisles of Toys 'R' Us." Gail
Johnson, "Consumers 'R' Us," *Adbusters*, Summer 1998, page 20.

70   "chemical giant Monsanto sics its legal team on anyone . . . " "Monsanto's
Legal Thuggery," *Food & Water Journal*, Summer 1998, page 10.

70   "A Fox TV affiliate . . ." Steve Wilson, "Fox in the Cow Barn," *The Nation*,
June 8, 1998, page 20. See also Jim Boothroyd, *Adbusters*, Winter 99,
page 20.

70   "The MAI would effectively create a single global economy . . . " Craig Cox,
"A Magna Carta for Multinationals," *Utne Reader*, November 1997, page 16.

75   "Nine out of ten North American women feel bad about some aspect of
their bodies . . . " *An Introduction to Food and Weight Problems*, National
Eating Disorder Information Centre, Toronto, 1985, page 5.

75   "A 1992 survey of eleven- to fifteen-year-old Canadian girls revealed that
50 percent thought they should be thinner." *The Health of Canada's Youth*,
Health and Welfare Canada, 1992.

75   "Now girls as young as five are watching what they eat." Donna Ciliska,
Why Diets Fail (Second Story Press, 1994), page 80.

75   "50 percent of them are on a diet." "The War Within," *Calgary Herald*,
October 6, 1997, page B5.

75   "violin deformity." Elizabeth Haiken, *Venus Envy: A History of Cosmetic
Surgery* (John Hopkins, 1998), pages 299–300.

75   "batwing disorder." Ibid.

75   "Some models have removed their bottom ribs to accentuate the thinness
of their waists." Sunday *New York Times*, Home News, December 1995.

78   "Every three hours a new McDonald's opens somewhere in the world."
      Richard Gibson, *Wall Street Journal*, January 22, 1996.

78   "The company spends over $1 billion every year on advertising." *Advertising Age*, September 28, 1998, page s4.

79   "The United States is the fattest nation on Earth . . . " Humphrey Taylor,
      president, Louis Harris and Associates, *American Demographics*, October
      1991, page 10.

79   "Flight attendants sometimes use Diet Coke . . . " Air Canada's in-flight
      crews quickly learn that while all soft drinks work as drain cleaners to
      some extent, Diet Coke works best, according to a friend who was a flight
      attendant with the airline until 1993.

82   Jane Holtz Kay, *Asphalt Nation* (Crown Publishers, 1997).

85   "The Global Economic Pyramid Scheme." Parts of this chapter were
      first published as "Voodoo at the Summit," in *Adbusters*, Summer 1997,
      page 18.

86   "Ecologically speaking, the world is already 'full' . . . " William E. Rees,
      "Sustainability, Growth, and Employment: Towards an Ecologically Stable,
      Economically Secure, and Socially Satisfying Future," University of British
      Columbia, School of Community and Regional Planning, a paper pre-
      pared for the International Institute for Sustainable Development, June
      1994, page ii.

87   "There are no . . . limits to the carrying capacity of the Earth . . . " Lawrence
      Summers, quoted by William E. Rees and Mathis Wackernagel, *Investing in
      Natural Capital: The Ecological Economics Approach to Sustainability*, A-M
      Jannson, M. Hammer, C. Folke and R. Costanza, editors (Island Press,
      1994), page 363.

87   "If it is easy to substitute other factors for natural resources . . . " Robert
      Solow, quoted by William E. Rees and Mathis Wackernagel, *Investing
      in Natural Capital: The Ecological Economics Approach to Sustainability*,
      page 365.

87   "We have in our hands—in our libraries really—the technology . . . " Julian
      Simon, *The State of Humanity: Steadily Improving*, Cato Policy Report
      17:5, Washington, D.C., The Cato Institute, 1995.

87   William E. Rees and Mathis Wackernagel, *Our Ecological Footprint: Reducing Human Impact on the Earth* (New Catalyst, 1995).

87   "40 percent of terrestrial and 25 percent of marine photosynthesis have now been diverted to human use." Rees, "Sustainability, Growth, and Employment," page 1.

88   Robert Ayres, "Limits to the Growth Paradigm," *Journal of the International Society for Ecological Economics* (1996), 19:117–134.

88   For a compelling discussion of the shortcomings of the GDP as a measure of progress, see "If the Economy Is Up, Why Is America Down?" by Clifford Cobb, Ted Halstead and Jonathon Rowe, *The Atlantic Monthly*, October 1995. See also Kalle Lasn, "The Economics of the Last Hurrah," *Adbusters*, Volume 1, Number 3, page 65.

89   "Conducting economic policy based soly on the GDP is like driving your car without a gas gauge." Ronald Coleman, professor of political science at St. Mary's University, on CBC radio program, *As It Happens*, November 24, 1997.

89   "A more accurate measure of economic progress." Herman Daly and John Cobb, Jr., *For the Common Good, Redirecting the Economy Towards Community, the Environment, and a Sustainable Future* (Beacon Press, 1989), page 401.

90   "The difference between science and economics . . . " Ferdinand E. Banks, from a lecture he gave in Australia in 1989. His *Energy Economics: A Modern Introduction* will be published by Uppsala Economic Studies in 1999.

92   "creating $50 in play money for every $1 worth of real products . . . " Joel Kurtzman, *The Death of Money* (Simon & Schuster, 1993), page 65. The quote actually reads: " . . . major actors in the global economy . . . play with $20 to $50 (no one knows for sure) in the financial economy for every $1 in the real economy . . . "

93   "Trillions of dollars slosh around this system . . . " Richard Longworth, *Global Squeeze—The Coming Crisis for First World Nations* (Contemporary Books, 1998).

93   "97 percent of the world's monetary transactions . . . " personal communication from Michel Chossudovsky, University of Ottawa. See also Patrick Harrison, "The Revolution Will Be Carbonated," *Adbusters*, Autumn 1998, page 65.

Spring

99 "The Revolutionary Impulse" The primary inspiration for this chapter and the Situationist strain throughout this book came from: Greil Marcus, *Lipstick Traces—A Secret History of the Twentieth Century* (Harvard University Press, 1989); Len Bracken, *Guy Debord—Revolutionary* (Feral House, 1997); Guy Debord, *Comments on the Society of Spectacle* (Verso, 1990); *Situationist International Anthology*, edited and translated by Ken Knabb (Bureau of Public Secrets, 1981); Raul Vaneigem, *The Revolution of Everyday Life* (Rebel Press/Left Bank Books, 1994); Guy Debord, *The Society of Spectacle* (Zone Books, 1994), Simon Sadler, *The Situationist City* (The MIT Press, 1998) and Sadie Plant, *The Most Radical Gesture* (Routledge, 1992). Start your journey with Marcus or Plant and then move on to some of the original Situationist texts in Knabb's anthology. See Ken Knabb's website: <www.slip.net/~knabb> for a few Situationist texts.

99 "one word of truth sounds like a pistol shot." Czeslaw Milosz, in his acceptance speech for the 1980 Nobel Prize for literature.

101 "putting switches on the street lamps . . . " the Lettrist International, quoted by Greil Marcus, *Lipstick Traces—A Secret History of the Twentieth Century* (Harvard University Press, 1989), page 411.

101 " 'a moral, poetic, erotic, and almost spiritual refusal' to cooperate with the demands of commodity exchange." Sadie Plant, *The Most Radical Gesture* (Routledge, 1992), page 8.

101 "the 'spectacle' of modern life." Guy Debord, *The Society of Spectacle* (Zone Books, 1994). Originally published in France as *La société du spectacle* (Buchet-Chastel, 1967).

102 On *"dérive,"* see Guy Debord, "Theory of the Derive," Knabb, page 50. See also Bracken, page 66; Marcus, pages 168, 170; and Plant, pages 58–59.

102 For one of the most striking Situationist texts on the subject of cities and *dérive,* see Ivan Chtcheglov, "Formulary for a New Urbanism," 1953, in *Situationist International Anthology*, edited and translated by Ken Knabb (Bureau of Public Secrets, 1981). I first read "Formulary for a New Urbanism" at: <www.slip.net/~knabb>.

102 "locomotion without a goal." Plant, page 58.

103 On "playful creation" of "situations," see Guy Debord, "Report on the Construction of Situations and on the International Situationist Tendency's Conditions of Organization and Action," Knabb, pages 17–25.

103 On *"détournement"* see Guy Debord and Gil J. Wolman, "Methods of Détournement," Knabb, page 8; "Détournement as Negation and Prelude," Knabb, page 55; Plant, pages 86–89; and Marcus, pages 168, 170, 179, 372.

103 "radically reinterpreting world events such as the 1965 riots in Los Angeles . . . " See "The Decline and Fall of the Spectacle-Commodity Economy," *Internationale Situationniste* #10, March 1966, Knabb, pages 153–160.

103 "a famous drawing of Lenin . . . " See a picture of this drawing in Bracken, page 64.

103 "the deadly diversion of the force of life in favor of an empty heaven . . ."; "God is dead . . ." For a full translation of this sermon, see Bracken, pages 10–11.

103 "devalue the currency of the spectacle." Marcus, page 179.

104 "a gigantic turning around of the existing social world." Plant, page 89.

104 "Even the tiniest of gestures . . . " Plant, page 67.

104 "a new poetry of real experience and a reinvention of life are bound to spring." Raul Vaneigem, *The Revolution of Everyday Life* (Rebel Press/Left Bank Books, 1994), quoted by Plant, page 67.

104 "the citizens of the most advanced societies on earth, thrilled to watch whatever it is they're given to watch." Marcus, page 99.

105 "provisional and lived." The Situationists, quoted by Marcus, page 175.

105 "the "bizarre" quarter, the "sinister" quarter, the "tragic" quarter . . . " Ivan Chtcheglov, in Knabb, page 1.

105 "I wrote much less than most people who write, but drank much more than most people who drink." See Bracken, page viii.

105 "our kind will be the first to blaze a trail into a new life." Karl Marx, adopted by Guy Debord, and quoted by Marcus, page 185.

105 "believe in faster trains and more traffic . . . " L.T.C. Rolt, *High Horse Riderless* (G. Allen & Unwin, 1947).

106 "Generations of poets, prophets, and revolutionaries, not to mention lovers, drug-takers . . . " Plant, page 39.

108 "The détournement of the right sign, in the right place at the right time . . . "
Marcus, page 179.

108 "would leave nothing to chance." Gil Wolman, quoted by Marcus, page 358.

112 *"fin de millénium* atmosphere of postmodernity." Plant, page 5.

114 "Establishment and Resistance in one convenient package." Tom Frank,
Commodify Your Dissent: Salvoes from the Baffler (Norton, 1977), page 35.

114 Juliet B. Schor, *The Overspent American—Upscaling, Downshifting, and the
New Consumer* (Basic Books, 1998).

114 Hal Niedzviecki, "Are We Really Depressed?—Introducing Malaise Culture," *Broken Pencil,* Issue 5, November 1997, page 14.

118 "Allen Ginsberg, who found that . . . " Rick Salutin, *The Globe and Mail,*
May 16, 1997, page C1.

119 "Project Censored." Sonoma State University, http://censored.sonoma.edu/
ProjectCensored/.

119 "Lewis Lapham . . . steadfastly refused to be drawn into the debate." The
invitation to debate "the ethical and moral ramifications of running
tobacco ads" came in an open letter to Lewis H. Lapham in *Adbusters,*
Summer 1994, page 79. Lapham's first "response" appeared in *Adbusters,*
Winter 1995, page 91. Then, "The Ball's in Your Court Now Lewis,"
Adbusters, Summer 1995, page 62. Lapham's second "response" appeared
in *Adbusters,* Fall 1995, page 5, and his comments to *The Globe and Mail,*
in *Adbusters,* Winter 1995, page 5. Further thrusts and parries in *Adbusters,*
Spring 1996.

121 "a ruthless criticism of all that exists." Karl Marx, 1843, adopted by the Situationists, and quoted by Marcus, page 175.

121 "We will wreck this world." *Internationale Situationniste* #1, June 1958,
quoted by Marcus, page 175.

123 "The Meme Wars." The title of this chapter is taken from Kalle Lasn, "The
Meme Wars," *Adbusters,* Autumn 1998, pages 6 and 7.

123 The word "meme" was coined by evolutionary biologist Richard Dawkins
in *The Selfish Gene* (Oxford University Press, 1976). Derived from a Greek
root meaning "to imitate," the word describes how memes mimic the

behavior of genes, propagating not body to body but "by leaping from brain to brain."

123 The term "meme warfare" was coined by Paul Spinrad in *Adbusters,* Winter 1995, page 40.

123 "a guerrilla information war." Marshall McLuhan, *Culture Is Our Business* (Ballantine Books, 1970), page 66.

130 *Limits to Growth,* Donella Meadows, Dennis L. Meadows, Jorgen Randers, William W. Behrens III et al. (Universe Books, 1972).

130 "The manager of a housing co-op was . . . " I first read this story in an article titled "Places to Intervene in a System," by Donella Meadows, in *Whole Earth,* Winter 1997, page 82.

Summer

Many of the activist strategies in this part were originally published in *Adbusters, Blueprint for a Revolution* issue, Autumn 1998, and subsequent issues.

139 "Whadd'ya got?" Marlon Brando in *The Wild One,* 1954, directed by László Benedek.

140 "slave component." Sadie Plant, *zeroes + ones: digital women + the new technoculture* (Fourth Estate, 1997), page 4.

143 "Lying is the major form of human stress . . . " Brad Blanton, *Radical Honesty* (Dell, 1996), page xxv (preface).

145 "Sovereign people do not beg of, or negotiate with subordinate entities . . ." "When a subordinate entity violates . . . " Richard Grossman, "The Relationship of Humans to Corporations," an article he submitted to *Adbusters* in February 1997.

149 "Marshall McLuhan's World War III . . . " See Marshall McLuhan, *Culture Is Our Business* (Ballantine Books, 1970), page 66.

150 "Reframe Debates." This section was inspired by a story that Paul Cienfuegos, founding director, Democracy Unlimited of Humboldt County, told me circa May 1997.

154 "How much harm does a company have to do before we question its right to exist?" Paul Hawken, *The Ecology of Commerce—A Declaration of Sustainability* (HarperBusiness, 1993).

157 "A corporation has no heart, no soul, no morals." This idea is taken from Professor David R. Loy, *A Buddhist Critique of Transnational Corporations* (Professor in the Faculty of International Studies, Bunkyo University, Chigasaki, Japan; <www.igc.apc.org/bpf/think.html>).

160 "revoke the charter of the Standard Oil Trust of New York." Richard L. Grossman and Frank T. Adams, *Taking Care of Business—Citizenship and the Charter of Incorporation* (1993, Charter, Ink., P.O. Box 806, Cambridge, MA 02140), page 17.

160 "The state of Pennsylvania revoked the charters of a number of banks . . ." Ibid.

160 "Michigan, Ohio and New York revoked the charters of . . ." Ibid.

160 "In 1890, the highest court in New York State revoked . . . " Grossman, "The Relationship of Humans to Corporations."

160 "In 1976, U.S. Supreme Court Justices White, Brennan and Marshall noted that . . . " Ibid.

160 "In May 1998, New York Attorney General Dennis Vacco . . . " *The Wall Street Journal*, May 4, 1998, page A8. See also Randy Ghent, *Adbusters*, Autumn 1998, page 58.

160 "In Alabama . . . Judge William Wynn . . . " Randy Ghent, "Alabama Judge Threatens Big Tobacco," *Adbusters*, Winter 1999, page 54.

161 "On September 10, 1998, in what may be . . . " Randy Ghent, "Lawyers Guild Petition to Shut Down Unocal," *Adbusters*, Winter 1999, page 54.

161 "And . . . in the fiercely political university town of Arcata, California . . . " Randy Ghent, *Adbusters*, Winter 1999, page 51.

161 "centrally planned by global megacorporations"? David C. Korten, *The Post-Corporate World—Life After Capitalism* (Berrett-Koehler Publishers, Inc., 1999), page 1.

169 Faith Popcorn, *The Popcorn Report* (HarperCollins, 1992).

169 Duane Elgin, *Voluntary Simplicity—Toward a Way of Life That Is Out-wardly Simple, Inwardly Rich* (revised edition, William Morrow, 1993).

169 Vicki Robin and Joe Dominguez, *Your Money or Your Life: Transforming Your Life and Achieving Financial Independence* (Viking, 1992).

169 " ... The aggregate level of American life fulfillment ... " See also *Yearning for Balance—Views of Americans on Consumption, Materialism, and the Environment,* prepared for the Merck Family Fund by The Harwood Group, July 1995.

171 Juliet B. Schor, *The Overspent American—Upscaling, Downshifting, and the New Consumer* (Basic Books, 1998).

172 E. F. Schumacher, *Small Is Beautiful: A Study of Economics as If People Mat-tered* (Blond and Briggs, 1973).

172 Frances Moore Lappé, *Diet for a Small Planet* (Ballantine Books, 1991).

174 Brewster Kneen, *Invisible Giant—Cargill and Its Transnational Strategies* (Pluto Press, 1995). See also Brewster Kneen, "Taking On the Food Giants," *Adbusters,* Spring 1997, page 18.

174 "The average pound of food ... " Lynette Lamb, "Are Fresh Fruits and Veg-etables Really Healthy?" *Utne Reader,* Number 23.

175 "Over 50 percent of the calories in this Big Mac come from fat." From www.mcdonalds.com, McDonald's website.

176 "the most profoundly disturbing campaign in TV history." Bob Garfield, "Publicity Monster Turns on Klein," *Advertising Age,* September 4, 1995, page 18.

179 "Several high-profile architects ... " See Moshe Safdie with Wendy Kohn, *The City After the Automobile—An Architect's Vision* (Stoddart, 1997).

180 "Your private automobile will cost you ... " For an accounting of the social and environmental costs of automobiles see *Transportation Cost Analysis: Techniques, Estimates and Implications,* Victoria Transport Policy Institute, Todd Litman, director, litman@islandnet.com.

185 "Media Carta." Parts of this chapter first appeared in *Adbusters,* Winter 1999, pages 16–29.

186 "The great power of these organizations lies in their vertical integration ..."
     This idea came from Richard Masur, president of the Screen Actors Guild,
     The Nation, June 8, 1998, page 30.

188 David Grossman, *On Killing: The Psychological Cost of Learning to Kill in
     War and Society* (Little, Brown, 1995).

188 "Every time the story gets to a higher level, it's killed." David Grossman in
     a telephone interview with Bruce Grierson, September 7, 1998.

188 "Without fail, remorse or hesitation ..." Grossman-Grierson interview.

189 "The broadcasters may be powerful enough ... " Grossman-Grierson
     interview.

189 "Parents of the shooter ... " Grossman-Grierson interview.

194 Paul Klite, executive director, Rocky Mountain Media Watch. See Jerry M.
     Landay, "Getting a Movement Going," *The Nation*, June 8, 1998, page 10.
     See also Jim Boothroyd, *Adbusters*, Winter 1999, pages 26, 27.

196 " ... one of America's most powerful litigators ... " Talk with Stephen
     Rohde in March 1998.

197 " ... a high-profile Los Angeles media attorney and former president
     of the Beverly Hills Bar Association ... " Talk with Barry Shanley in
     March 1998.

197 Aldous Huxley, *Brave New World* (Coles Publishing Co., 1994).

201 "Redefining Progress" is the name of the San Francisco think tank that
     pioneered the Genuine Progress Indicator (GPI). Their *Community Indi-
     cators Handbook* helps communities start their own economic well-being
     indicators projects. <www.rprogress.org> (415) 781-1191.

201 "the human experiment on Planet Earth is veering out of control ... " This
     idea was taken from *World Scientists, Warning to Humanity*, by the Union
     of Concerned Scientists (UCS), April 1993.

202 "First we kill all the economists ... " This "How To Break the Neoclassical
     Trance" strategy first appeared as "How to Break the Voodoo Spell,"
     Adbusters, Summer 1997, page 25.

204 Thomas S. Kuhn, *The Structure of Scientific Revolutions* (University of Chicago Press, 1962, 1970).

204 "Kuhn's most profound insight . . . grabs the old-school practitioners by the scruffs of their necks and throws them out of power." Taken from Kalle Lasn, "Voodoo Economics," *Adbusters,* Volume 1, Number 3, page 57.

206 "A particularly effective economics teach-in was held at the University of Victoria . . . " "It feels like someone's telling you, 'You're stupid . . . " "There's no social security in a world that consumes the biosphere . . . " "Nuclear energy is touted as . . . " This story was taken from Jim Munroe, "Students Give Teachers a Failing Grade," *Adbusters,* Winter 1996, pages 32, 33.

Epilogue: The Millennial Moment of Truth

211 On "millennial moment of truth . . . ," see more in-depth discussion, Kalle Lasn, "Editor's Blast," *Adbusters,* Spring 1998, page 6.

212 "the most advanced urban transportation system is not the automobile but . . . *the bicycle, . . . shingle on your roof, . . . a good shade tree.*" These three ideas were taken from Ed Ayres, editor, *WorldWatch* magazine, September 1998, page 3.

213 "a chain reaction of refusal . . . " Len Bracken, *Guy Debord—Revolutionary* (Feral House, 1997), pages 174–175.

213 "*Enragés.*" For a description of the role that this group of radicals played in the 1968 Paris riots, see Bracken, pages 157–175.

213 "*Live Without Dead Time*" See *On the Poverty of Student Life,* by the members of the Situationist International and the students of Strasbourg University, *Situationist International Anthology,* edited and translated by Ken Knabb (Bureau of Public Secrets, 1981), page 337.

213 "Art students demanded the realisation of art; music students called for 'wild and ephemeral music'; footballers . . . " Sadie Plant, *The Most Radical Gesture* (Routledge, 1992), page 98.

213 "the largest general strike that ever stopped the economy of an advanced industrial country, and the first *wildcat general strike* in history . . . " *Internationale Situationniste* #12, September 1969, *Situationist International*

Anthology, translated by Ken Knabb (Bureau of Public Secrets, 1981), page 225.

213 "At the height of the uprising in Paris's Latin Quarter . . . three thousand took to the streets in Rome. Three days later . . . " Bracken, pages 174–175.

214 "The Beginning of an Epoch." The title of an article in *Internationale Situationniste* #12, September 1969, Knabb, pages 225–256.

214 "The death rattle of the historical irrelevants . . . " Zbigniew Brzezinski, quoted by Greil Marcus, *Lipstick Traces* (Harvard University Press, 1989), page 32.

214 "incessant technological renewal; integration of state and economy; generalized secrecy; unanswerable lies; an eternal present." Guy Debord, *Comments on the Society of Spectacle* (Verso, 1998), pages 11, 12.

Graphic Credits

Index

Page numbers in *italics* refer to illustrations.

About the Author

I was born in Tallinn, Estonia, during the middle of World War II, and spent my childhood years in a German displaced persons camp. When I was seven, my family immigrated to Australia, where I later earned a B.Sc. in pure and applied mathematics from the University of Adelaide. My first job was with the Australian Defense Department playing computer-simulated war games in the Pacific Ocean. While I was on a trip to Europe to find my roots, my boat stopped over in Yokohama; I fell in love with Japan and was unable to get back on the boat. I started a market research company in Tokyo, made a lot of money, traveled the world, and finally returned to Japan to marry Masako Tominaga. In 1970, we immigrated to Vancouver, Canada, where I started a film commune. Over the next few years, my experimental shorts and documentaries were broadcast on PBS, on CBC and around the world, winning over fifteen international awards.

In 1989, my work in film led to an epiphany. I produced a thirty-second TV spot about the disappearing old-growth forests of the Pacific Northwest, then discovered to my dismay that no TV station would sell me any airtime. Since then I've been fighting the human rights battle of our information age: the battle for the right to communicate, to receive and impart ideas and information through any media, regardless of frontiers. The *Media Foundation*, *Adbusters* magazine, *Powershift Advertising Agency* and the *Culture Jammers Network*—my projects for the past ten years—all stem from that moment's realization: that there is no democracy on the airwaves.

The Culture Jammers Network

We are a loose global network of artists, activists, writers, students, educators and entrepreneurs who want to launch the new social activist movement of the information age. Our aim is to topple existing power structures and forge a major shift in the way we will live in the twenty-first century. We believe culture jamming will become to our era what civil rights was to the '60s, what feminism was to the '70s, what environmental activism was to the '80s. It will alter the way we live and think. It will change the way information flows, the way institutions wield power, the way TV stations are run, the way the food, fashion, automobile, sports, music and culture industries set their agendas. Above all, it will change the way we interact with the mass media and the way meaning is produced in our society.

FIND OUT MORE ABOUT US
Visit the Culture Jammers Campaign Headquarters:
www.adbusters.org

TALK TO US
Call (604)736-9401, fax (604)737-6021 or write:
Adbusters Media Foundation
1243 West 7th Avenue
Vancouver, B.C. V6H 1B7, Canada

JOIN THE NETWORK
Put your e-mail address on our listserv and receive news
releases, campaign bulletins and strategic updates:
jammers@adbusters.org

SUBSCRIBE TO *ADBUSTERS* MAGAZINE
Phone 1-800-663-1243
or e-mail: subscriptions@adbusters.org